# WELCOME TO MY TABLE

## JEANNIE JACOBS

# WELCOME TO MY TABLE

For information, permissions, or bulk purchases, contact:

## Just Jeannie

Houston, Texas
www.justjeanniejacobs.com

Book design - Sheila Jackson

Laura Sanz - Cover Photography

Food photography and videos - Cat on The Table

Natalie D'Onofrio- Photography for tablescape photos

Cover design by Asym Haroon

Printed in the United States of America

**ISBN: 979-8-9926784-3-7 - Paperback**

**ISBN: 979-8-9926784-2-0 - Hardcover**

**First Edition**

# To my husband,

## Joseph

"Your unwavering love, strength, and belief in me have carried me through every season, every pivot, and every dream I've dared to chase. You are the calm in my chaos, the reason behind my courage, and the quiet force that keeps our family rooted and thriving. This book is a reflection of the life we've built—one filled with flavor, connection, and intentional joy.

Thank you for always pulling up a seat at my table.
With all my heart"

*Jeannie*

# TABLE OF CONTENTS

# TABLE OF CONTENTS CONT.

Welcome To My Table

# Welcome To My Table:

## Where Food and Life's Best Moments Happen

*Welcome to My Table* was inspired by the women I grew up around. My grandmother, aunties and close family friends transformed entertaining into an art. They had an incredible talent for making people feel special, whether it was through a lavish dinner party with waitstaff or a simple, intimate gathering. I witnessed how their thoughtful gestures created lasting connections and memories. Their influence instilled in me the belief that entertaining well isn't about wealth but about using creativity and thoughtfulness to help guests feel welcomed.

At four years old, I didn't understand why my aunties and grandmother invested so much time and care into entertaining. I thought people came just for the food. As I grew up, I realized it was so much more than that. It wasn't just about what was on the table—it was about how you made people feel while they were at the table.

Even at that young age, I was mesmerized by the women in my life. I wanted to be just like them, so I would mimic their every move. As they dressed to the nines for their gatherings, I would raid their closets, donning jewelry, outfits far too big for me, and even a wig or two! I felt so grown and important, ready to entertain in my "fancy" outfit.

My aunties took great pride in their homes and hosted with a keen sense of awareness for making people feel valued. They paid attention to the smallest details—learning a guest's favorite flower or interest, curating seating arrangements that encouraged connection, and setting the mood with music, lighting and scents. They believed that hospitality was an extension of love, and I saw firsthand how these small, thoughtful efforts created bonds that turned strangers into lifelong friends. This upbringing shaped my philosophy: hosting is less about extravagance and more about intention and heart.

Looking back, I realize I wasn't just playing dress-up, I was absorbing the values they modeled: making others feel special, connecting with care, and using creativity to elevate every experience. These early memories are the foundation of my love for hosting. I learned that when you bring people together, the details, the ambiance, the thoughtfulness, and the effort all become the story. And it's those stories that leave a lasting imprint far beyond the meal itself.

This book is a guide to elevating your everyday entertaining with thoughtful touches, clever styling tips, and heartfelt ideas that anyone can implement—no matter the budget. It's filled with inspiration to help you curate unforgettable gatherings, from a cozy brunch with friends to an elegant dinner party. You'll also find my personal anecdotes and lessons learned from watching my family turn ordinary moments into extraordinary experiences.

I want you to focus on thoughtful details rather than extravagance. Creating a warm and inviting atmosphere with lighting, music and scents is essential. Don't forget to use what you have, whether flowers from your yard, an eclectic mix of tableware, or a pre-made meal creatively presented. Ambiance is everything, so light a few candles, play music that lifts the mood, and use scents to create a relaxing atmosphere. Even a small gesture, like a personalized welcome note or a guest book, can make someone feel incredibly special. It's about being intentional and creating a space that invites connection.

Also, take time to learn something meaningful about your guests and incorporate it into the gathering. Simple things like their favorite drink or a unique seating arrangement add a personal touch. Greeting guests with a welcome beverage or light bites tailored to their taste and perhaps a handwritten note at their place setting can make a big impact. Spending time getting to know your guests before the event starts allows you to create moments behind the scenes that truly resonate.

*Welcome To My Table* combines recipes, tablescape ideas and personal stories to show readers how entertaining can be both approachable and extraordinary. Each section offers practical tips alongside heartfelt anecdotes to inspire readers to create their own connections and joy. It's about turning the ordinary into something memorable and celebrating the beauty of life's small experiences.

# ABOUT ME

Growing up, family dinners—especially Sunday after church and during holidays—were sacred. As I worked hard studying medicine and began my career as a physician, those traditions fell by the wayside. I was consumed by work, often on call during holidays, and a disconnect in my own family life formed. One day, while working on a holiday, I realized I didn't want to miss these special moments anymore.

From that point on, I became intentional about reclaiming Sundays and special occasions. I refused to work on holidays and began creating dining experiences that rivaled some of the fanciest restaurants, simply because I could, and it brought joy to my family and friends.

These moments inspired the recipes and ideas in this book—many rooted in old family traditions, but also influenced by my adventurous spirit for trying new cuisines, from Indian to Mexican and even Nigerian dishes. This book reflects the belief that food is a bridge to connection, renewal and joy.

My personal journey has taught me that food is more than sustenance; it's a way to connect and create memories. I've reestablished Sunday family dinners as a cornerstone of my life. These meals are more than just time to eat; they're moments to reflect, renew and strengthen the bonds within my family and community. I've also made a point to celebrate both the big and small moments in life—over-the-top birthday parties for my children, holiday dinners that bring loved ones together and even special touches on ordinary days, like showing up at school with treats or planning impromptu family movie nights.

These traditions remind us that it's okay to celebrate ourselves, to smile, shout and sing our own praises. They've taught my children that joy comes not only from grand events but also from the smaller, thoughtful moments that make life beautiful.

My family's traditions revolved around food, togetherness and making people feel cherished. Sunday dinners after church and holiday meals were epic events where everyone gathered, talked, laughed and shared. My grandmother and aunties didn't just cook—they curated experiences. They set the mood with music, scents and thoughtful touches that made everyone feel special.

These traditions taught me that it's the effort and intention behind the event that matter, not how much money you spend. My aunties could take flowers from the yard or mix traditional and modern tableware to create magic. They also wove storytelling into their gatherings, inspiring creativity and deeper connections. These values shape the way I entertain today, whether it's a simple weeknight meal or an elaborate holiday celebration.

Creating your own traditions is essential because they ground you in what matters most—connection, love and community. Traditions give us something to look forward to, a sense of stability and memories that carry us through life's ups and downs. They're also a way of expressing who you are and what you value.

When you create traditions, you're not only building meaningful moments for yourself but also leaving a legacy for others. These moments teach your family, friends and even your children to celebrate life, honor relationships and find joy in the everyday. Whether it's as simple as a weekly family dinner or as elaborate as a holiday feast, traditions bring people together, nurture bonds and create stories worth remembering.

*Jeannie Jacobs*

www.justjeanniejacobs.com

# BITES OF BLISS

# BITES OF BLISS

Appetizers are more than just a prelude to the main course—they're the gateway to the dining experience. They awaken the palate, stir anticipation and set the stage for what's to come. A thoughtful appetizer isn't just food; it's an expression of care and creativity, signaling the tone and expectations for the entire meal. Whether it's a casual gathering or an elegant dinner party, these small bites create an ambiance of excitement, encourage connection and set the mood for an unforgettable evening.

I learned this firsthand during a family vacation in Italy. My children, who rarely touched bruschetta at home, fell head over heels for it there. The simplest ingredients—juicy, vine-ripened tomatoes, fresh basil, garlic and crusty bread—created pure magic. My son exclaimed, "The tomatoes burst in my mouth like I was eating them straight off the vine!"

It wasn't just the taste but the freshness and simplicity that left an impression. That night, the bruschetta became the star of the evening and taught me an invaluable lesson: when made with love and the freshest ingredients, even the simplest dishes can leave the most lasting impressions.

Appetizers also offer an opportunity for creativity and variety. They allow the chef to showcase an array of flavors and textures—sweet and salty, creamy and crunchy, tangy and savory—all in small, delightful bites. They drive social interaction, encouraging guests to mingle and connect before the main course. And most importantly, they can be as simple or as sophisticated as you want them to be.

The secret to creating showstopping appetizers lies in three things: freshness, presentation and creativity. Start with high-quality ingredients like seasonal produce or artisanal cheeses. Layer flavors and textures—a crisp, crunchy base with a velvety topping, garnished with something fresh and vibrant. And don't overlook presentation: colorful garnishes, beautiful serving pieces and thoughtful arrangements can transform simple bites into edible works of art.

Pairing appetizers with drinks adds another layer of magic to the experience. Match the intensity of flavors—light, delicate bites pair beautifully with crisp white wines or sparkling water, while bolder flavors call for fuller-bodied reds or craft cocktails. Complement flavors, too: spicy dishes pair wonderfully with off-dry wines like Riesling, and salty bites shine alongside a glass of Champagne. Don't be afraid to experiment; a citrusy mocktail paired with tangy ceviche can create an unexpected yet delightful pairing.

Appetizers may be small, but their impact is mighty. They introduce your guests to the dining experience, spark conversation and elevate your gathering into something truly special. With a little thought and creativity, these light bites can become the highlight of any occasion.

# ALOO TIKKI SLIDERS

*Serves 4-6*

## INGREDIENTS

**For the Aloo Tikki (Potato Patties):**

3 medium potatoes, boiled and mashed

¼ cup green peas, boiled and

mashed slightly

2 tablespoons bread crumbs

½ teaspoon cumin powder

½ teaspoon garam masala

½ teaspoon red chili powder

Salt to taste

1 tablespoon oil (for frying)

**For Assembling the Sliders:**

Mini buns or pav bread

2 tablespoons butter (for toasting)

Tamarind chutney

Mint chutney

Thinly sliced red onion

## INSTRUCTIONS

1. **Prepare the Aloo Tikki:**
   In a mixing bowl, combine mashed potatoes, green peas, bread crumbs, cumin powder, garam masala, red chili powder and salt.
   Mix well and shape into small round patties about the size of the mini buns.

2. **Cook the Aloo Tikki:**
   Heat 1 tablespoon oil in a pan over medium heat.
   Fry the patties for 3-4 minutes per side or until golden brown and crispy.
   Remove and drain on a paper towel.

3. **Toast the Mini Buns:**
   Slice the buns in half.
   Heat butter in a pan and toast the buns until golden and slightly crispy

4. **Assemble the Sliders:**
   Spread tamarind chutney on one side of the bun and mint chutney on the other.
   Place a crispy aloo tikki in the center.
   Top with thinly sliced red onions.
   Cover with the top bun and gently press down.

5. **Serve Immediately:**
   Enjoy warm with extra chutneys or a side of spicy masala fries.

## PRO TIPS FOR THE BEST ALOO TIKKI SLIDERS:
Use fresh bread crumbs for a crispier patty.
For extra crunch, coat patties in dry bread crumbs before frying.
Toast the buns well to prevent them from getting soggy.
Add cheese or lettuce for a fun variation.

## SERVING SUGGESTION:
Serve sliders on a platter with small bowls of extra chutneys for dipping.

# CHARRED SHISHITO PEPPERS WITH SEA SALT & LEMON

*Serves 4-6*

## INGREDIENTS

1 pound shishito peppers

1 tablespoon olive oil

Flaky sea salt to taste

Lemon wedges for serving

## INSTRUCTIONS

1. **Preheat the Skillet:**
   Heat a cast-iron skillet or heavy-bottomed pan over high heat until very hot.

2. **Char the Peppers:**
   In a bowl, toss the shishito peppers with olive oil, ensuring they are evenly coated.
   Add them to the hot skillet in a single layer. Let them cook undisturbed for 1-2 minutes until blistered.
   Stir occasionally and continue cooking for 5-7 minutes until all sides are charred and the peppers are tender.

3. **Season and Serve:**
   Remove from heat and sprinkle immediately with flaky sea salt.
   Transfer to a serving dish and serve with lemon wedges for squeezing over the top.

## PRO TIPS FOR THE BEST CHARRED SHISHITO PEPPERS:
Use high heat to achieve the perfect blister without overcooking.
Do not overcrowd the pan—cook in batches if needed for even charring.
Toss the peppers right before serving to keep them crisp and flavorful.
Occasionally, a shishito pepper is extra spicy—warn your guests for a fun surprise!

## SERVING SUGGESTION:
As an Appetizer: Serve alongside a creamy aioli, spicy sriracha mayo or miso dipping sauce.
With a Charcuterie Board: Pair with cheese, nuts, and olives for a rustic spread.
In a Main Dish: Use them as a topping for rice bowls, grilled meats or tacos.
With a Cold Drink: Enjoy with a chilled white wine, crisp lager or a citrusy mocktail.

**Watch Video!**

SHISHITO PEPPERS

JUST JEANNIE

Bites of Bliss

# FIG AND GOAT CHEESE CROSTINI

*Serves 8-10*

## INGREDIENTS

1 baguette, sliced

4 ounces goat cheese

4 fresh figs, sliced

2 tablespoons honey

1 teaspoon fresh thyme leaves

1 tablespoon olive oil (for toasting)

Salt and black pepper to taste

## INSTRUCTIONS

1. **Toast the Baguette:**
   Preheat oven to 375°F (190°C).
   Arrange baguette slices on a baking sheet and brush lightly with olive oil.
   Toast for 8-10 minutes until golden and crisp.

2. **Assemble the Crostini:**
   Spread goat cheese evenly over the toasted baguette slices.
   Top with fresh fig slices.

3. **Finish with Flavor:**
   Drizzle with honey and sprinkle with fresh thyme leaves.
   Season with a pinch of salt and black pepper to enhance the flavors.

4. **Serve Immediately:**
   Arrange on a serving platter or wooden board and enjoy.

## PRO TIPS FOR THE BEST CROSTINI:

Use high-quality goat cheese for a smoother, richer taste. Let it come to room temperature for easy spreading.

For extra crispiness, toast the baguette under the broiler for 1 - 2 minutes. Watch carefully to prevent burning.

Add depth by roasting the figs in the oven at 375°F for 10 minutes to enhance their sweetness.

Balance the flavors by adding a pinch of flaky sea salt after drizzling the honey.

Bake ahead: Toast the baguette slices in advance and store them in an airtight container. Assemble just before serving.

## SERVING SUGGESTION:

**Charcuterie Board Addition:** Serve alongside cured meats like prosciutto or salami for a sweet and salty contrast.

**With Wine:** Pair with a crisp Sauvignon Blanc, a light Pinot Noir or a sparkling Prosecco to complement the flavors.

**Brunch Spread:** Serve with fresh fruit, yogurt, and a side of scrambled eggs for an elegant breakfast option.

**Holiday Appetizer:** Arrange on a wooden board with fresh herbs and edible flowers for a festive touch.

## TWISTS & VARIATIONS:

**Savory Touch:** Add a drizzle of balsamic glaze for a tangy contrast.

**Crunch Factor:** Sprinkle crushed pistachios, walnuts or toasted almonds for texture.

**Sweet & Salty:** Top with crispy prosciutto or Serrano ham for a salty balance.

**Creamier Flavor:** Mix goat cheese with cream cheese or ricotta for an extra smooth spread.

**Seasonal Swap:** Use roasted grapes, pears or apples instead of figs for a different take.

# POMEGRANATE - GLAZED LAMB LOLLIPOPS

*Serves 4*

## INGREDIENTS

8 lamb chops, frenched

½ cup pomegranate molasses

2 tablespoons honey

1 tablespoon balsamic vinegar

½ teaspoon garlic powder

1 teaspoon fresh mint, chopped

Salt to taste

## INSTRUCTIONS

1. **Toast the Baguette:**
   Season and Grill the Lamb:
   Season lamb chops with salt and garlic powder.
   Grill over medium-high heat for 3-4 minutes
   per side for medium-rare or until desired
   doneness.

2. **Prepare the Glaze:**
   In a small saucepan, combine pomegranate
   molasses, honey and balsamic vinegar.
   Simmer over medium heat for 3-5 minutes,
   stirring occasionally until slightly thickened.

3. **Glaze the Lamb:**
   Brush the warm glaze over the grilled lamb
   chops just before serving.

4. **Garnish and Serve:**
   Sprinkle with fresh mint and serve immediately.

## PRO TIPS FOR THE BEST LAMB LOLLIPOPS:
Let the lamb rest for 5 minutes before serving to retain juices.
Use a meat thermometer for perfect doneness (130°F for medium-rare).
Serve with roasted vegetables or a couscous salad for a complete meal.

## SERVING SUGGESTION:
Arrange on a platter with a side of fresh pomegranate seeds and mint sprigs.

Welcome To My Table

# SIP & SAVOR

# SIP & SAVOR

Thoughtfully crafted drinks elevate any meal by engaging the senses—taste, aroma and visuals. A well-made cocktail or mocktail not only complements the dishes on the menu but also balances flavors and textures while adding a touch of sophistication.

I served Hurricane Cocktails at my Mardi Gras-themed wedding reception. I was sure this drink would steal the spotlight. I was so wrong! Instead, my signature Almond Iced Tea mocktail became the unexpected highlight of the evening. Guests couldn't stop raving about its unique flavor; the subtle almond essence paired beautifully with lemon and pineapple juice, transforming a classic Southern iced tea into something extraordinary. The chef had to prepare multiple batches to keep up with the demand from 600 guests! That experience taught me that a thoughtfully crafted mocktail can rival any cocktail, leaving a lasting impression that guests won't forget.

Drinks set the tone for the meal, signaling attention to detail and quality. They also foster interaction and conversation, creating a sense of connection among guests. Offering both alcoholic and non-alcoholic options ensures everyone feels included, making the celebration more welcoming and inclusive.

When crafting drinks, I focus on three key elements: flavor balance, presentation and inclusivity. Using fresh, seasonal ingredients guarantees vibrant flavors and appealing aesthetics. I love creating unique combinations of fruits, herbs and spices while keeping the drinks approachable. Thoughtful touches like homemade syrups, infused ice or fragrant garnishes elevate the experience. Most importantly, I always include crafted mocktails, ensuring every guest, regardless of their preference for alcohol, feels part of the celebration.

Seasonal ingredients are at the heart of memorable beverages, bringing superior taste and a connection to the time of year. Fresh, ripe fruits and herbs naturally enhance flavor and add visual appeal. Seasonal elements also make drinks feel special and unique to the occasion. For instance, a peach mojito in the summer offers a refreshing burst of sweetness, while a chai latte martini in the fall delivers warmth and coziness.

Welcome to My Table

**Here are a few creative twists on classic beverages:**
  **Chai Latte Martini:** A spiced, warming variation of the classic espresso martini.
  **Peach Mojito:** A summer-fresh take on the mint mojito, enhanced with juicy peach purée.
  **Ginger-Lime Sparkler:** A zesty twist on the Moscow Mule, made with ginger syrup and sparkling water.
  **Rosemary Paloma:** A fragrant upgrade to the traditional Paloma, featuring rosemary-infused simple syrup.

These twists honor the essence of classic drinks while adding new dimensions of flavor and aroma that surprise and delight guests.

Designing a drink menu starts with understanding the theme, menu and ambiance of the event. For a summer garden party, I might serve a Peach Mojito for a refreshing burst, a Lavender Lemonade for elegance, and a Rosemary Paloma for an herbal twist. Pairing flavors is key; light, crisp cocktails complement seafood, while bold, rich options suit heartier fare.

Presentation is just as important. Beautiful glassware, colorful garnishes, and creative serving pieces can transform a simple drink into a work of art. And don't forget descriptive language words like "zesty," "refreshing," or "smooth" add intrigue and set the stage for an unforgettable experience.

# ALMOND ICED TEA

*Serves about 6*

## INGREDIENTS

4 cups water

4 black tea bags

1/4 cup granulated sugar

6-8 ounces pineapple juice

(adjust based on preference)

1/2 cup fresh lemon juice

1 tablespoon almond extract

(adjust to taste)

Ice cubes

Lemon slices and fresh mint for garnish

## INSTRUCTIONS

1. Bring the water to a boil in a saucepan.

2. Remove from heat and add the black tea bags. Let steep for 5 minutes.

3. Discard the tea bags and stir in the sugar until fully dissolved. Allow the tea to cool to room temperature.

4. Stir in the pineapple juice, lemon juice and almond extract. Taste and adjust the almond extract as needed—add more if a stronger almond flavor is desired.

5. Fill glasses with ice cubes and pour the almond iced tea over the ice.

6. Garnish with lemon slices and fresh mint.

### PRO TIP:
Use fresh-squeezed pineapple juice for the best flavor. Let the tea chill in the fridge for a few hours before serving to allow the flavors to blend beautifully.

### SERVING SUGGESTION:
Serve in tall glasses over ice with a decorative straw, a mint sprig and a thin lemon wheel. Pair this drink with tropical-inspired dishes like grilled chicken skewers, fresh fruit platters or coconut shrimp for a complete summer vibe.

Welcome to My Table

# PEACH BLOSSOM (COCKTAIL)

## *Serves 1*

## INGREDIENTS

1 ounce peach schnapps

1 ounce peach nectar

4 ounces chilled sparkling wine

(Prosecco or Champagne)

Fresh peach slices, for garnish

Mint sprigs, for garnish

## INSTRUCTIONS

1. **Prepare the Glass:**
   Chill a champagne flute or coupe glass in the freezer for a few minutes before serving.

2. **Mix the Base:**
   Pour peach schnapps and peach nectar into the glass.
   Gently stir to combine.

3. **Add the Sparkle:**
   Top with chilled sparkling wine and let the bubbles mix naturally.

4. **Garnish and Serve:**
   Garnish with a fresh peach slice and a mint sprig.
   Serve immediately.

## PRO TIPS FOR THE BEST PEACH BLOSSOM COCKTAIL:

Use fresh, ripe peaches for a naturally sweet garnish and enhanced flavor.
Chill all ingredients beforehand to keep the drink crisp and refreshing.
For a floral touch, add a splash of elderflower liqueur or garnish with an edible flower.
For a stronger cocktail, add ½ ounce of vodka or white rum.

## NON-ALCOHOLIC VERSION (MOCKTAIL TWIST):

Substitute peach schnapps with peach juice.
Replace sparkling wine with sparkling water or ginger ale.

## SERVING SUGGESTIONS:

Presentation: Serve in a chilled champagne flute or coupe glass for a sophisticated touch.
Pairings: Enjoy with light appetizers like fresh fruit skewers, charcuterie or mini goat cheese tarts for a summery pairing.

**Watch Video!**

PEACH BLOSSOM

JUST JEANNIE

Sip & Savor

# GINGER LIME SPARKLER (MOCKTAIL)

*Serves 1*

## INGREDIENTS

**For the Drink:**

1 ounce ginger syrup (recipe below)

Juice of 1 lime (freshly squeezed)

4 ounces sparkling water

Ice cubes

Lime wedge, for garnish

**For the Ginger Syrup:**

½ cup water

½ cup sugar

2 tablespoons fresh ginger, sliced

## INSTRUCTIONS

**Make the Ginger Syrup:**

1. In a small saucepan, combine water, sugar, and sliced ginger over medium heat.

2. Stir until the sugar dissolves completely.

3. Simmer for 5-7 minutes, then remove from heat.

4. Let the syrup steep for 10-15 minutes for a stronger ginger flavor.

5. Strain out the ginger and let the syrup cool before using. Store in an airtight container in the refrigerator for up to 2 weeks.

**Make the Ginger Lime Sparkler:**

1. **Prepare the Glass:**
   Fill a highball or rocks glass with ice cubes.

2. **Mix the Drink:**
   Pour ginger syrup and fresh lime juice into the glass.
   Stir well to combine.

3. **Add Sparkling Water:**
   Top with sparkling water and stir lightly.

4. **Garnish and Serve:**
   Garnish with a lime wedge.
   Serve immediately.

## PRO TIPS FOR THE BEST GINGER LIME SPARKLER:

For a spicier kick, muddle fresh ginger with lime juice before adding syrup.
Use honey instead of sugar in the syrup for a natural sweetness.
For a cocktail version, add vodka or bourbon for a refreshing twist.
For extra depth, use ginger beer instead of sparkling water.
Chill all ingredients beforehand for the coldest, most refreshing drink.

# ROSEMARY PALOMA (COCKTAIL/MOCKTAIL)

*Serves 1*

## INGREDIENTS

**For the Drink:**

2 ounces grapefruit juice (freshly squeezed for best flavor)

1 ounce rosemary simple syrup (recipe below)

2 ounces soda water (or tequila for a cocktail version)

Ice cubes

Rosemary sprig, for garnish

Grapefruit slice, for garnish (optional)


**For the Rosemary Simple Syrup:**

½ cup water

½ cup sugar

2 sprigs fresh rosemary

## INSTRUCTIONS

**Make the Rosemary Simple Syrup:**

1. In a small saucepan, combine water, sugar and rosemary sprigs over medium heat.

2. Stir until the sugar dissolves completely.

3. Let simmer for 5 minutes, then remove from heat.

4. Allow the syrup to steep for 15 minutes for a stronger rosemary flavor.

5. Strain out the rosemary and let the syrup cool before using. Store in an airtight container in the refrigerator for up to 2 weeks.

**Make the Rosemary Paloma:**
   Fill a highball or rocks glass with ice cubes.

2. **Mix the Drink:**
   Pour grapefruit juice and rosemary simple syrup over the ice.
   Stir gently to combine.

3. **Add the Sparkle:**
   Top with soda water for a mocktail or tequila for a cocktail.
   Stir lightly.

4. **Garnish and Serve:**
   Garnish with a rosemary sprig and an optional grapefruit slice.
   Serve immediately.

## PRO TIPS FOR THE BEST ROSEMARY PALOMA:

Use fresh grapefruit juice for the most vibrant flavor.
For extra citrusy brightness, rub the rim of the glass with grapefruit zest.
Adjust sweetness by adding more or less rosemary syrup to taste.
For a smoky twist, use mezcal instead of tequila.
Chill the glass before serving for an extra refreshing drink. Garnish with a rosemary sprig.
Torch the rosemary sprig slightly for a smoky aroma.

**Watch Video!**

ROSEMARY PALOMA

JUST JEANNIE

Sip & Savor

# PINEAPPLE MOJITO (COCKTAIL/MOCKTAIL)

*Serves 1*

## INGREDIENTS

½ cup fresh pineapple chunks

6 fresh mint leaves

Juice of 1 lime

1 ounce white rum (substitute soda water

for mocktail)

Club soda

Ice cubes

Mint sprig for garnish

## INSTRUCTIONS

1. **Muddle the Ingredients:**
   In a tall glass, add pineapple chunks, mint leaves and lime juice.
   Use a muddler or the back of a spoon to gently mash the ingredients, releasing the juices and mint oils.

2. **Add the Base:**
   Pour in rum (or soda water for a mocktail) and stir well to combine.

3. **Top with Club Soda:**
   Fill the glass with ice cubes and top with club soda.
   Stir lightly to mix.

4. **Garnish and Serve:**
   Garnish with a mint sprig and an optional pineapple wedge.
   Serve immediately.

## PRO TIPS FOR THE BEST PINEAPPLE MOJITO:

Use fresh pineapple juice instead of chunks for a smoother texture and bolder flavor.
For extra sweetness, add a splash of simple syrup or honey if needed.
Chill your glass beforehand for an extra refreshing drink.
Make it a frozen mojito by blending all ingredients with ice.
For a tropical twist, add a splash of coconut water

**Watch Video!**

PINEAPPLE MOJITO

JUST JEANNIE

Sip & Savor

SOULSCAPE
COCONUT & SOY BLEND SCENTED CANDLE
2 oz / 56 g

SOULSCAPE
COCONUT & SOY BLEND SCENTED CANDLE
8 oz / 226 g

*Welcome To My Table*

32

# SPICED PEAR SPRITZER (MOCKTAIL)

## Serves 1

## INGREDIENTS

**For the Mocktail:**

1 cup pear juice

½ ounce cinnamon syrup (see below)

Sparkling water

Ice cubes

Pear slice, for garnish

Cinnamon stick (optional, for garnish)

**For the Cinnamon Syrup:**

½ cup water

½ cup sugar

2 cinnamon sticks

## INSTRUCTIONS

**Make the Cinnamon Syrup:**
1. In a small saucepan, combine water, sugar and cinnamon sticks over medium heat.

2. Stir until the sugar fully dissolves.

3. Simmer for 5 minutes, then remove from heat.

4. Let the syrup steep for 15 minutes to infuse more cinnamon flavor.

5. Strain out the cinnamon sticks and allow the syrup to cool before using. Store in an airtight container in the refrigerator for up to 2 weeks.

**Make the Spiced Pear Spritzer:**
1. **Prepare the Glass:**
   Fill a tall glass with ice cubes.

2. **Mix the Base:**
   Pour pear juice and cinnamon syrup into the glass.
   Stir gently to combine.

3. **Add the Sparkle:**
   Top with sparkling water and stir lightly.

4. **Garnish and Serve:**
   Garnish with a pear slice and, if desired, a cinnamon stick for extra aroma.
   Serve immediately.

## PRO TIPS FOR THE BEST SPICED PEAR SPRITZER:

Chill the pear juice beforehand for a crisp, refreshing taste.
For more spice, add a pinch of nutmeg or clove to the cinnamon syrup.
Use flavored sparkling water like vanilla or ginger for added depth.
Turn it into a cocktail by adding bourbon or spiced rum.

# MORNING SPARK

Welcome To My Table

# MORNING SPARK

Brunches have surged in popularity, especially post-COVID, as people are seeking opportunities to reconnect in meaningful ways. Brunches offer a relaxed yet celebratory vibe that brings together the best of breakfast and lunch, catering to a variety of tastes and dietary needs. It strikes the perfect balance between casual and elegant, allowing hosts and guests to enjoy the day without feeling rushed. More than just a meal, brunch has become a joyful blend of delicious food, great company, and treasured moments.

One of my favorite brunches was a Christmas Eve gathering I hosted for my children and their friends. The festive decor set the stage, with a table adorned in seasonal colors, thoughtful decorations, and small favors that sparked meaningful conversations about holiday traditions and childhood memories. The menu was simple yet elevated, with vibrant dishes that delighted everyone—from the smallest guests to their parents. Mini Santa-shaped pancakes, prepared ahead of time, were the standout, allowing me to spend more time enjoying the celebration instead of being stuck in the kitchen. The event was a success because it captured the essence of togetherness and joy.

### Planning a Stress-Free Brunch

Hosting a successful brunch starts with preparation. Create your menu well in advance and shop early for the freshest ingredients. Dishes like casseroles or baked goods can be prepped the day before, significantly reducing stress. Don't shy away from incorporating high-quality, store-bought items—mini pancakes, pastries or pre-made sauces save time without sacrificing quality. Setting up self-serve stations for food and beverages keeps the flow of the event smooth and allows guests to help themselves while warming trays ensure dishes stay at the perfect temperature. Delegate small tasks, like refilling drinks or setting the table, so you can focus on hosting. Finally, create a warm and inviting atmosphere with fresh flowers, twinkle lights, and soft music that sets the tone for a memorable gathering.

### Crafting a Perfectly Balanced Menu

A well-rounded brunch menu satisfies both savory and sweet cravings. Balance the spread by pairing dishes like quiche or frittata with indulgent options like waffles or French toast. Add variety with lighter dishes, such as a fresh fruit salad or yogurt parfaits, to complement heartier fare. Incorporate proteins like smoked salmon, vegetarian breakfast sausages or eggs to give the menu substance and appeal. Seasonal ingredients elevate the flavors—roasted vegetables for savory dishes or berry compote for sweet treats.

### Elevating Your Brunch Setup

Elevate your gathering by creating a themed experience that ties everything together, whether it's a Christmas brunch adorned with elves and twinkle lights or a summer garden party with floral accents. Add a playful touch by using nontraditional serving ideas, such as placing a dish in a decorative planter surrounded by fresh flowers or designing themed displays for kids. To keep the setup functional and stylish, create dedicated stations for food and beverages. Elevate the beverage station with elegant containers, like carafes for juices or glass dispensers for syrups, adding a sophisticated touch. Layer your decor with fresh flowers, candles, and pieces from around your home to create depth and texture, while twinkle lights add a magical glow. Don't overlook the power of music—curate a playlist or hire live musicians to enhance the ambiance and make your event truly unforgettable.

**Listen Now!**

SPOTIFY PLAYLIST

JUST JEANNIE

Morning Spark

# ARUGULA SALAD WITH PEAR

*Serves 4*

## INGREDIENTS

4 cups fresh arugula

1 ripe pear, thinly sliced

¼ cup walnuts, toasted

¼ cup crumbled blue cheese or goat cheese

2 tablespoons olive oil

1 tablespoon balsamic vinegar

1 teaspoon honey

Salt and pepper to taste

## INSTRUCTIONS

1. In a bowl, whisk together olive oil, balsamic vinegar, honey, salt and pepper.

2. Toss the arugula, pear slices, and walnuts in the dressing.

3. Sprinkle with crumbled cheese.

4. Serve immediately.

PRO TIP:
Add grilled chicken for a heartier salad, or swap pears for apples for a fall variation.

**Watch Video!**

ARUGULA SALAD

JUST JEANNIE

Morning Spark

# SEAFOOD BREAKFAST TACOS

*Makes 4 tacos*

## INGREDIENTS

4 corn tortillas

6 oz cooked shrimp or crab meat

4 eggs, scrambled

½ avocado, diced

¼ cup queso fresco or shredded cheese

2 tablespoons fresh cilantro, chopped

Salt & pepper to taste

¼ teaspoon smoked paprika

Salsa or hot sauce for serving

## INSTRUCTIONS

1. Warm tortillas in a dry skillet.

2. Season scrambled eggs with smoked paprika.

3. Layer tortillas with eggs, seafood, avocado and cheese.

4. Garnish with cilantro and serve with salsa.

## PRO TIP:
Use smoked salmon instead of shrimp for a different flavor profile.

# GARLIC BUTTER STEAK & CHIMICHURRI WITH EGGS

*Serves 2*

## INGREDIENTS

**For the Steak:**

1 lb ribeye, skirt steak or flank steak

1 tablespoon olive oil

1 tablespoon butter

3 cloves garlic, minced

1 teaspoon smoked paprika

½ teaspoon ground cumin

½ teaspoon chili flakes (optional, for heat)

Salt and black pepper to taste

**For the Chimichurri Sauce:**

½ cup fresh parsley, finely chopped

¼ cup fresh cilantro, finely chopped (optional)

3 cloves garlic, minced

½ teaspoon red pepper flakes (adjust to taste)

½ teaspoon oregano

1 teaspoon red wine vinegar

Juice of ½ lemon

½ cup olive oil

Salt and black pepper to taste

**For the Eggs:**

2-4 large eggs

1 tablespoon butter

Salt and black pepper

## INSTRUCTIONS

**Make the Chimichurri Sauce:**

1. In a bowl, mix parsley, cilantro (if using), garlic, red pepper flakes, oregano, red wine vinegar and lemon juice.

2. Slowly whisk in the olive oil until the sauce is well combined.

3. Season with salt and black pepper to taste. Let it sit for at least 10 minutes to allow the flavors to meld.

**Prepare the Steak:**

1. Pat the steak dry with a paper towel, then season with smoked paprika, cumin, salt, black pepper and chili flakes.

2. Heat olive oil in a cast-iron skillet over medium-high heat until shimmering.

3. Add the steak and sear for 3-4 minutes per side (depending on thickness and preferred doneness).

4. During the last minute of cooking, add butter and minced garlic, basting the steak continuously.

5. Remove from heat and let the steak rest for 5 minutes before slicing.

**Cook the Eggs:**

1. Heat butter in a non-stick pan over medium heat.

2. Crack the eggs into the pan and cook to your preferred doneness (sunny-side-up, over-easy or scrambled).

3. Season with salt and black pepper.

## PRO TIPS:

For extra flavor, let the steak marinate in olive oil, garlic and spices for 30 minutes to an hour before cooking.

Want a smokier taste? Use a grill instead of a skillet and char the steak over high heat. For a creamy contrast, serve with avocado slices or crumbled queso fresco.

Looking for a spicy kick? Add a drizzle of hot honey or a dash of smoked chipotle powder to the eggs.

**Watch Video!**

CHIMICHURRI

JUST JEANNIE

Morning Spark

# CLASSIC QUICHE LORRAINE

*Serves 6-8*

## INGREDIENTS

1 store-bought or homemade pie crust

6 large eggs

1 cup heavy cream

1 cup Gruyère cheese, shredded

½ cup cooked bacon or ham, diced

¼ teaspoon nutmeg

Salt and black pepper to taste

## INSTRUCTIONS

1. **Preheat the Oven:**
   Preheat oven to 375°F (190°C).
   Roll out the pie crust into a 9-inch pie dish or tart pan, pressing it evenly along the edges.
   Blind bake the crust by pricking it with a fork, lining it with parchment paper and filling it with pie weights or dried beans
   Bake for 10 minutes, then remove the weights and bake for another 5 minutes until lightly golden.

2. **Prepare the Egg Mixture:**
   In a bowl, whisk together eggs, heavy cream, nutmeg, salt and black pepper until smooth.

3. **Assemble the Quiche:**
   Evenly spread Gruyère cheese and cooked bacon or ham over the baked crust.
   Pour the egg mixture over the filling, ensuring everything is evenly distributed.

4. **Bake the Quiche:**
   Bake for 35-40 minutes or until the center is set and slightly golden.
   A knife inserted into the middle should come out clean.

5. **Rest and Serve:**
   Let the quiche rest for 10 minutes before slicing for cleaner cuts.

### Vegetarian Option:

Replace bacon or ham with one of the following:
½ cup sautéed mushrooms and spinach
½ cup caramelized onions and roasted red peppers
½ cup chopped asparagus and leeks

### Pro Tips for the Best Quiche Lorraine:

Use cold butter if making a homemade crust for extra flakiness.
Blind baking prevents a soggy bottom and keeps the crust crisp.
For a deeper flavor, let the quiche cool slightly before serving.
Shred cheese fresh instead of using pre-shredded for better melting.

### SERVING SUGGESTIONS:

Serve warm with a light green salad and a simple vinaigrette.
Pair with fresh fruit for a brunch-friendly meal.
Enjoy with a glass of crisp white wine like Chardonnay or Sauvignon Blanc.

# HERB-CRUSTED CHEDDAR BISCUITS

*Makes 10–12 biscuits*

## INGREDIENTS

2 cups all-purpose flour

1 tablespoon baking powder

½ teaspoon salt

½ cup unsalted butter, cold and cubed

1 cup shredded cheddar cheese

1 tablespoon fresh thyme (or 1 teaspoon dried)

¾ cup buttermilk

2 tablespoons melted butter (for brushing, optional)

## INSTRUCTIONS

1. **Preheat the Oven:**
   Preheat oven to 400°F (200°C). Line a baking sheet with parchment paper.

2. **Mix Dry Ingredients:**
   In a large bowl, whisk together flour, baking powder, and salt.

3. **Cut in Butter:**
   Add cold cubed butter and use a pastry cutter or your fingers to mix until the dough resembles coarse crumbs.

4. **Add Cheese and Herbs:**
   Stir in cheddar cheese and thyme until evenly distributed.

5. **Incorporate Buttermilk:**
   Gradually add buttermilk, stirring until just combined. Do not overmix.

6. **Shape and Bake:**
   Drop heaping spoonfuls of dough onto the prepared baking sheet.
   Bake for 12-15 minutes or until biscuits are golden brown.

7. **Finish with Butter:**
   Brush the warm biscuits with melted butter before serving.

Welcome To My Table

## PRO TIPS FOR PERFECT BISCUITS:

Use cold butter to create flaky layers.
Don't overmix the dough to keep the biscuits light and tender.
For extra flavor, mix garlic powder into the dough or the melted butter.
Chill the dough for 10 minutes before baking for a better rise.

## SERVING SUGGESTIONS:

Serve warm with butter, honey or jam.
Pair with soups, stews or chili for a comforting meal.
Use as a savory breakfast sandwich base with eggs and bacon.

## TWISTS ON THIS RECIPE:

Garlic and Herb: Add ½ teaspoon garlic powder for extra savory flavor.
Spicy Kick: Mix in ½ teaspoon cayenne pepper or diced jalapeños.
Bacon Cheddar Biscuits: Stir in ¼ cup cooked, crumbled bacon.
Parmesan Rosemary: Swap cheddar for Parmesan and thyme for rosemary.

**Watch Video!**

**CHEDDAR BISCUITS**

JUST JEANNIE

# WHITE CHOCOLATE BREAD PUDDING WITH WHITE CHOCOLATE RUM SAUCE

*Serves 8-10*

## INGREDIENTS

**For the Bread Pudding:**

1 loaf brioche or French bread, cubed (preferably day-old)

3 cups heavy cream

1 cup whole milk

1 ½ cups white chocolate chips or chopped white chocolate

½ cup granulated sugar

½ cup brown sugar

4 large eggs

2 teaspoons vanilla extract

½ teaspoon cinnamon

¼ teaspoon nutmeg

¼ teaspoon salt

¼ cup melted butter

**For the White Chocolate Rum Sauce:**

1 cup heavy cream

½ cup whole milk

½ cup white chocolate chips

¼ cup granulated sugar

2 tablespoons dark rum (or bourbon)

1 teaspoon vanilla extract

1 tablespoon butter

**Optional Toppings:**

Powdered sugar

Toasted pecans

Fresh berries

## INSTRUCTIONS

**Make the Bread Pudding:**

1. Preheat oven to 350°F. Grease a large baking dish with butter.

   In a saucepan over medium heat, combine heavy cream and milk. Stir occasionally until it just begins to steam (don't let it boil).

   Remove from heat and stir in white chocolate chips, mixing until smooth.

   In a large bowl, whisk together eggs, sugars, vanilla, cinnamon, nutmeg and salt.

   Slowly whisk in the melted white chocolate mixture until well combined.

   Place the bread cubes in a large bowl. Pour the custard mixture over the bread and let sit for 10 minutes, allowing the bread to soak up all that deliciousness.

   Transfer the soaked bread mixture into the greased baking dish, drizzle with melted butter and bake for 40-45 minutes or until the top is golden brown and the custard is set.

2. **Make the White Chocolate Rum Sauce:**

   In a saucepan over medium heat, combine heavy cream, milk, sugar and white chocolate chips. Stir constantly until the chocolate is melted and the sauce thickens slightly.

   Remove from heat and stir in rum (or bourbon), vanilla extract and butter until smooth.

3. **Serve & Indulge:**

   Let the bread pudding cool for 5-10 minutes, then drizzle with warm white chocolate rum sauce.

   Dust with powdered sugar, sprinkle with toasted pecans and serve with fresh berries for an extra touch.

## PRO TIPS:

Use day-old bread for better texture—it soaks up the custard without getting mushy.

For extra richness, add ½ cup white chocolate chunks to the bread mixture before baking.

Make it boozier! Add a splash of bourbon to the custard for a deep, caramelized flavor.

For a crispy top, broil for the last 2 minutes, watching carefully so it doesn't burn.

**Watch Video!**

**BREAD PUDDING**

JUST JEANNIE

Morning Spark

# TABLE FOR TWO

# TABLE FOR TWO

A romantic night at home is the perfect blend of simple yet meaningful elements: new recipes, heartfelt notes, soft candlelight and your favorite music—topped off with the cozy comfort of a movie and treats. By prepping in advance and incorporating personal touches, you can turn an ordinary evening into a heartfelt celebration, whether it's Valentine's Day or just an anytime moment to connect. Even amidst busy schedules and family responsibilities, this intimate gesture serves as a beautiful reminder of why you value each other and how love can be celebrated in the simplest, most special ways.

As busy professionals, my husband and I often find it tough to carve out time for romantic date nights—especially around Valentine's Day when restaurants are packed and everything feels rushed. So, we started a tradition of planning intimate, cozy dinners at home. One of my favorite evenings came from leaning into this tradition: we skipped the crowds and created a personalized, indulgent experience that felt all the more special because it was just for us.

We started by brainstorming a "wish list" for dinner. Sometimes, we go all out and cook from scratch; other times, we splurge on a chef or pick up a ready-made feast from a favorite local market. For Valentine's a few years ago, we settled on cooking rosemary-garlic lamb chops—a dish we'd been wanting to try for ages. To keep things simple, we added light yet flavorful appetizers to the mix, like a small charcuterie board and a crisp salad. What really made the night stand out, though, were the small, heartfelt touches: I placed handwritten notes around the house and under our plates, each one a little reminder of what our relationship means to us. That night reminded me that it's not just about the food—it's about the connection, the thoughtfulness and the joy of creating something meaningful together.

Crafting a romantic dinner begins with a personalized menu. Start by discussing what you both truly crave or wish to experience, ensuring the meal feels special and unique rather than an ordinary dinner at home. For appetizers, keep it light—opt for a fresh salad, a small charcuterie board or a few playful bites to spark your appetite without overshadowing the main course. When it comes to the entrée, let one dish shine as the "star" of the evening. Choose something you've never tried or rarely enjoy, like a gourmet lamb dish, homemade fresh pasta or a beautifully prepared seafood recipe. By focusing on these elements, your intimate meal becomes an unforgettable culinary experience.

Make your dessert or snacks the highlight of the evening with indulgent treats that feel both special and thoughtful. A decadent Chocolate Lava Cake is always a crowd-pleaser, with its warm, gooey center that's sure to impress. You can even pre-make the batter and bake it last minute, keeping things stress-free. For a perfect presentation, serve it with a dusting of powdered sugar or a handful of fresh berries for added color and flavor. If you're craving something creamy and luxurious, Panna Cotta or Crème Brûlée

are perfect choices. These desserts are rich and velvety, and the best part is that they can be prepared the night before, allowing you to relax before your romantic evening. If you're looking for something unique and interactive, consider creating a Dessert Board. This mini-tasting experience can include a selection of chocolates, fresh fruit and perhaps a special cheese or two. Tuck a hidden note or sweet message among the treats to make it a delightful surprise. No matter which dessert you choose, it's sure to end your evening on a sweet note.

### Candlelight, Music and a Movie for Two

Setting the mood is just as important as the meal itself when planning a romantic evening at home. Start by dimming the overhead lights and letting candles cast a warm, soft glow. A simple yet elegant floral arrangement or touch of greenery can elevate the table without overcomplicating the setup. Add personal touches to make the night feel even more special—tuck little love notes under napkins, next to wine glasses or even on mirrors for unexpected moments of delight.

To enhance the atmosphere, curate a playlist that fits the mood. Whether you're into smooth jazz or something more upbeat like hip hop, let the music set the tone while pairing it with a drink that complements the vibe—perhaps a bold red wine or a handcrafted cocktail. After dinner, extend the romance with a cozy movie night for two. Snuggle up on the couch with a special bowl of popcorn, jazzed up with gourmet seasonings and a stash of your favorite candies (even the ones you usually hide from the kids). This small indulgence turns an ordinary film into a shared experience that feels intimate and memorable.

### Prepping in Advance

In an effort to ensure a smooth and stress-free evening, prepping in advance is key. Start by planning your menu early. Decide whether you'll be cooking everything yourself, hiring a chef or opting for premade meals—this helps you organize your shopping list or place any necessary orders well in advance. Once the menu is set, break down the prep into stages. Marinate meats, assemble sauces and chop veggies earlier in the day so that you can focus on enjoying the evening rather than rushing through last-minute tasks.

Set the table and décor before you start cooking. Lay out the plates, silverware, candles, and any special touches, like a small floral arrangement or personalized place settings, so you can focus on the meal and your partner. Don't forget to choose the movie and treats ahead of time—select a film you'll both enjoy and stock up on gourmet popcorn or your favorite nostalgic candies. Being prepared ensures the evening flows effortlessly, allowing you both to relax and savor every moment.

Go-To Recipes with a "Wow" Factor and elevate an ordinary dinner into an extraordinary experience with these show-stopping recipes. These recipes not only impress but also keep preparation stress-free, allowing you to focus on the joy of sharing a memorable meal.

# ENTREES FOR TWO

Welcome To My Table

# HERB-CRUSTED SALMON WITH DILL SAUCE

*Serves 2*

## INGREDIENTS

**For the Salmon:**

2 salmon fillets (about 6 oz each)

½ cup panko breadcrumbs

2 tablespoon fresh parsley, finely chopped

1 tablespoon lemon zest

1 tablespoon olive oil

½ teaspoon salt

¼ teaspoon black pepper

**For the Dill Sauce:**

½ cup Greek yogurt

2 tablespoon fresh dill, finely chopped

1 tablespoon lemon juice

1 clove garlic, minced

¼ teaspoon salt

¼ teaspoon black pepper

## INSTRUCTIONS

1. **Preheat the Oven:**
   Preheat your oven to 400°F (200°C).
   Line a baking sheet with parchment paper or lightly grease it with oil.

2. **Prepare the Herb Crust:**
   In a small bowl, mix together panko breadcrumbs, parsley, lemon zest, olive oil, salt and black pepper  until well combined.

3. **Coat the Salmon:**
   Pat the salmon fillets dry with a paper towel. Place them skin-side down on the prepared baking sheet.
   Evenly press the herb-crumb mixture onto the top of each fillet, ensuring a thick, even layer.

4. **Bake the Salmon:**
   Transfer the baking sheet to the preheated oven. Bake for 12-15 minutes or until the salmon is cooked through and flakes easily with a fork. If desired, broil for the last 1-2 minutes to achieve a crispy golden crust.

5. **Prepare the Dill Sauce:**
   While the salmon is baking, whisk together Greek yogurt, fresh dill, lemon juice, minced garlic, salt and black pepper in a small bowl. Adjust seasoning if needed.

6. **Serve:**
   Remove the salmon from the oven and let it rest for 2-3 minutes.
   Plate the salmon and generously drizzle with dill sauce or serve it on the side.
   Garnish with extra dill or lemon wedges for a fresh finish.

PRO TIP:
Serve salmon with roasted asparagus or a light cucumber-dill salad.

SERVING SUGGESTION:
Garnish the salmon with lemon slices and dill sprigs.

DRINK PAIRING:
**Wine:** Crisp Chardonnay to complement the rich salmon and tangy dill. Non-Alcoholic: Sparkling water with lemon and mint.

# COQ AU VIN

*Serves 2-3*

## INGREDIENTS

4 bone-in, skin-on chicken thighs

4 strips bacon, chopped

1 cup dry red wine

1 cup chicken stock

1 cup mushrooms, sliced

1 cup pearl onions

2 cloves garlic, minced

2 sprigs fresh thyme

Salt and pepper to taste

## INSTRUCTIONS

1. **Cook Bacon:**
   In a Dutch oven, cook chopped bacon over medium heat until crispy.
   Remove with a slotted spoon and set aside.

2. **Sear Chicken:**
   Season chicken with salt and pepper.
   Sear in bacon fat until golden brown (about 5 minutes per side).
   Remove and set aside.

3. **Sauté Vegetables:**
   Add mushrooms, pearl onions and garlic to the pot.
   Cook until softened (3-5 minutes), then remove and set aside.

4. **Deglaze the Pot:**
   Pour in red wine, scraping up browned bits from the bottom.
   Let it simmer for 2 minutes to reduce slightly.

5. **Simmer the Dish:**
   Return chicken, bacon and vegetables to the pot.
   Add chicken stock and thyme.
   Bring to a simmer, cover and cook for 30-40 minutes until chicken is tender.

6. **Serve:**
   Discard thyme sprigs and serve warm with crusty bread or mashed potatoes.

PRO TIP:
Prepare the Coq au Vin a day ahead for flavors to meld beautifully.

SERVING SUGGESTION:
Plate the chicken with creamy mashed potatoes and pearl onions.

DRINK PAIRING:
**Wine:** A full-bodied Burgundy for depth and richness. Non-Alcoholic: Warm mulled grape juice for a cozy pairing.

**Watch Video!**

COQ AU VIN

JUST JEANNIE

Entrees for Two

# EGGPLANT PARMESAN STACK

*Serves 2-4*

## INGREDIENTS

1 large eggplant, sliced into ½-inch rounds

1 cup marinara sauce

1 cup mozzarella cheese, shredded

½ cup Parmesan cheese, grated

1 cup breadcrumbs (Italian-style recommended)

2 eggs, beaten

½ cup all-purpose flour

½ teaspoon salt

¼ teaspoon black pepper

½ teaspoon garlic powder (optional)

½ teaspoon Italian seasoning (optional)

Olive oil for frying

## INSTRUCTIONS

1. **Prepare the Eggplant:**
   Lightly salt the eggplant slices and let them sit for 15-20 minutes to draw out excess moisture. Pat them dry with a paper towel.

2. **Breading the Eggplant:**
   Set up three bowls: one with flour, one with beaten eggs, and one with breadcrumbs mixed with garlic powder and Italian seasoning (if using).
   Dredge each eggplant slice in flour, then dip it in the beaten eggs, and finally coat it with breadcrumbs.

3. **Frying the Eggplant:**
   Heat about ¼ inch of olive oil in a large skillet over medium heat.
   Fry the breaded eggplant slices in batches until golden brown, about 2-3 minutes per side.
   Transfer to a plate lined with paper towels to absorb excess oil.

4. **Assembling the Stacks:**
   Preheat oven to 375°F (190°C).
   In a baking dish, spread a thin layer of marinara sauce.
   Place one fried eggplant slice in the dish, spoon some marinara sauce over it, sprinkle with mozzarella and Parmesan.
   Repeat layering 2-3 times to create stacks.

5. **Baking the Stacks:**
   Bake uncovered for 20 minutes or until the cheese is melted and bubbly.

6. **Serving:**
   Let the stacks rest for 5 minutes before serving.
   Garnish with fresh basil or parsley, if desired.

## PRO TIPS FOR THE BEST EGGPLANT PARMESAN STACK:

**Pre-salt the Eggplant** – Sprinkle slices with salt and let them sit for 20-30 minutes to draw out excess moisture and bitterness. Pat dry before breading.

**Double Coat for Extra Crunch** – Dip in flour before the egg wash for a sturdier crust.

**Bake Instead of Frying** – For a lighter version, bake the breaded eggplant slices at 400°F for 20 minutes, flipping halfway.

**Use Fresh Mozzarella** – Instead of shredded, use thin slices of fresh mozzarella for a creamy, melty texture.

**Make it Ahead** – Bread and fry the eggplant in advance, then assemble and bake before serving.

**Let it Rest Before Serving** – Allow the stacks to sit for 5 minutes after baking to help them hold their shape.

**Drink pairing:** Chianti or Vermentino

**Mocktail options:** Sparkling Citrus Spritzer – Mix sparkling water with fresh orange juice and a splash of basil syrup for a refreshing pairing or Italian Soda with Pomegranate or Blood Orange.

# FILET MIGNON WITH PEPPERCORN SAUCE

*Serves 2*

## INGREDIENTS

2 filet mignon steaks (6-8 oz each)

2 tablespoon butter

1 teaspoon fresh thyme, chopped

1/2 teaspoon black pepper

1/2 teaspoon salt

1/2 cup beef broth

1 tablespoon Dijon mustard

1/2 teaspoon crushed peppercorns

1/2 cup heavy cream

1 tablespoon olive oil

## INSTRUCTIONS

1. Season filet mignon with salt, black pepper and thyme.

2. Heat olive oil in a pan over medium-high heat. Sear steaks for 3-4 minutes per side (for medium-rare) or until desired doneness.

3. Remove steaks from the pan and let them rest for 5 minutes to retain juices.

4. In the same pan, melt butter and add beef broth, Dijon mustard and crushed peppercorns. Stir well.

5. Simmer for 3-4 minutes, then lower the heat and stir in heavy cream. Cook for another 2 minutes until the sauce thickens slightly.

6. Serve filet mignon with the creamy peppercorn sauce drizzled over the top.

## SERVING SUGGESTION:
Plate steaks on a serving dish with a side of roasted vegetables or garlic mashed potatoes for a well-balanced meal.

## PRO TIP:
Let the steaks rest before slicing to ensure maximum juiciness. For extra depth of flavor, deglaze the pan with a splash of beef broth before adding the cream.

## Drink Pairing:
**Wine:** A full-bodied Burgundy for depth and richness. Non-Alcoholic: Warm mulled grape juice for a cozy pairing.

# DESSERTS FOR TWO

Welcome To My Table

84

# RASPBERRY CHEESECAKE MOUSSE

*Serves 2*

## INGREDIENTS

½ cup (4 oz) cream cheese, softened

1 teaspoon vanilla bean paste (or vanilla extract)

¼ cup powdered sugar

½ cup fresh raspberries, mashed (plus extra for garnish)

1 cup heavy whipping cream

1 tablespoon lemon juice (optional, for extra tartness)

Graham cracker crumbs (for garnish, optional)

## INSTRUCTIONS

1. **Prepare the Cream Cheese Mixture:**
   In a mixing bowl, beat the cream cheese, vanilla bean paste and powdered sugar with an electric mixer until smooth and creamy.

2. **Mash the Raspberries:**
   In a separate bowl, mash the raspberries using a fork until slightly chunky. For a smoother texture, strainout the seeds.
   Stir in the lemon juice, if using.

3. **Whip the Cream:**
   In another bowl, whip the heavy cream until stiff peaks form.

4. **Fold Everything Together:**
   Gently fold the whipped cream into the cream cheese mixture until fully combined.
   Add the mashed raspberries and fold again until incorporated.

5. **Chill and Serve:**
   Spoon the mousse into serving glasses or bowls. Refrigerate for at least one hour before serving for a firm texture.

6. **Garnish and Enjoy:**
   Top with extra raspberries and graham cracker crumbs for a cheesecake-like crunch.
   Serve chilled.

## PRO TIPS FOR THE PERFECT MOUSSE:

Use softened cream cheese for a smooth, lump-free texture.
Whip the cream to stiff peaks so the mousse stays light and airy.
Chill for at least an hour to allow the flavors to meld and set properly.
This mousse can be stored in the fridge for up to two days.

# CREME BRULEE

*Serves 4 (using 4 ramekins)*

## INGREDIENTS

2 cups heavy cream

½ cup sugar, divided

4 egg yolks

1 teaspoon vanilla extract

## INSTRUCTIONS

1. **Preheat the oven to 325°F (163°C):**
   Place four ramekins in a deep baking dish.

2. **Heat the Cream:**
   In a saucepan over medium heat, warm the heavy cream until it just starts to simmer. Do not let it boil.
   Remove from heat.

3. **Prepare the Egg Mixture:**
   In a mixing bowl, whisk together egg yolks and ¼ cup of sugar until pale and slightly thickened.

4. **Temper the Eggs:**
   Slowly pour the warm cream into the egg mixture while whisking constantly to prevent curdling. Stir in vanilla extract.

5. **Bake in a Water Bath:**
   Strain the mixture through a fine mesh sieve to remove any curdled bits, then divide evenly among the ramekins.
   Fill the baking dish with hot water halfway up the sides of the ramekins to create a water bath.
   Bake for 35-40 minutes or until the edges are set but the center is slightly jiggly.

6. **Cool and Chill:**
   Remove ramekins from the water bath and let them cool to room temperature.
   Refrigerate for at least 2 hours (preferably overnight) until fully set.

7. **Caramelize the Sugar:**
   Before serving, sprinkle 1-2 teaspoons of sugar evenly over each custard.
   Using a kitchen torch, caramelize the sugar until golden and crisp. If using the broiler, place ramekins under high heat for 1-2 minutes, watching carefully to prevent burning.

8. **Serve:**
   Let the sugar harden for a minute, then serve immediately.

PRO TIPS FOR THE BEST CREME BRULEE:
Use room-temperature egg yolks for a smoother custard.
Strain the mixture before baking for a silky texture.
Bake in a water bath to ensure even cooking and prevent cracking.
Chill thoroughly before torching to keep the custard firm.
Use superfine sugar for a more even caramelized crust.

**Watch Video!**

CRÈME BRÛLÉE

JUST JEANNIE

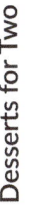

# MOLTEN CHOCOLATE LAVA CAKES

*Serves 4*

## INGREDIENTS

4 ounces semi-sweet chocolate, chopped

½ cup unsalted butter

2 large eggs

2 large egg yolks

½ cup powdered sugar

¼ cup all-purpose flour

Butter or cooking spray (for greasing ramekins)

## INSTRUCTIONS

1. **Preheat the Oven:**
   Preheat oven to 425°F (218°C).
   Grease four 6-ounce ramekins with butter or non-stick spray. Lightly dust with flour or cocoa powder for easy removal.

2. **Melt Chocolate and Butter:**
   In a heatproof bowl, melt the chopped chocolate and butter together.
   Use a double boiler or microwave in 20-second intervals, stirring in between until smooth.
   Set aside to cool slightly.

3. **Prepare the Batter:**
   In a separate bowl, whisk together eggs, egg yolks and powdered sugar until pale and slightly thickened.
   Slowly pour in the melted chocolate mixture, stirring continuously.

4. **Incorporate the Flour:**
   Gently fold in the flour using a spatula until just combined. Do not overmix.

5. **Fill and Bake:**
   Divide the batter evenly among the prepared ramekins.
   Bake for 10-12 minutes until the edges are set but the centers are still soft.

6. **Rest and Serve:**
   Let the cakes rest for 1 minute, then carefully invert onto plates. Serve warm with vanilla ice cream, whipped cream or fresh berries.

**Watch Video!**

MOLTEN CHOCOLATE

JUST JEANNIE

## PRO TIPS FOR PERFECT LAVA CAKES:

Use high-quality chocolate for a richer taste.
Do not overbake—the center should remain soft and gooey.
Grease the ramekins well to ensure easy release.
Chilling the batter for 30 minutes before baking helps control the lava consistency.

# AFFOGATO AL CAFFE

*Serves 2*

## INGREDIENTS

2 scoops vanilla gelato (or high-quality
vanilla ice cream)

½ cup hot espresso (or strong brewed
coffee)

## INSTRUCTIONS

1. **Prepare the Serving Glass:**
   Use a small glass, cup or dessert bowl to serve.

2. **Add the Gelato:**
   Place two scoops of vanilla gelato in the
   serving glass.

3. **Pour the Espresso:**
   Brew hot espresso (or strong coffee).
   Immediately pour it over the gelato.

4. **Serve Immediately:**
   Enjoy right away as the gelato melts into the
   coffee, creating a creamy, rich flavor.

## PRO TIPS FOR THE BEST AFFOGATO:

Use freshly brewed espresso for the best taste.
For a twist, add a splash of amaretto, Kahlúa or Frangelico.
Top with shaved chocolate, crushed biscotti or a drizzle of caramel for extra indulgence.

# GATHER & FEAST

# GATHER & FEAST

Hosting a gathering that accommodates dietary restrictions, diverse tastes and preferences while honoring tradition can be both rewarding and fulfilling. To ensure everyone feels included, I suggest offering a variety of options, such as a vegetarian-friendly salad or gluten-free grilled vegetables alongside a main course like fried chicken.

Customizable options, like serving sauces and dressings on the side, give your guests more control over their meals. Whenever possible, communicate with guests in advance to plan your menu and find suitable substitutes, like a dairy-free cheese for macaroni and cheese or a gluten-free crust for chicken pot pie. For example, when making our signature cornbread dressing, I create a gluten-free batch using specialty cornmeal and vegetable stock, ensuring that everyone can enjoy the flavors.

When planning a menu for a diverse group, it's important to balance traditional favorites with new or experimental dishes. For instance, pairing classic macaroni and cheese with a light, grilled veggie platter offers something for everyone. Consider complementary flavors. Rich dishes like chicken pot pie or cornbread dressing can be lightened up with a fresh salad or roasted vegetables. Offering multiple protein choices, such as chicken, shrimp or a vegetarian option like lentil stew, ensures there's something for all dietary preferences.

Our family's staple dishes—like chicken pot pie, macaroni and cheese, cornbread dressing and sweet potato soufflé with pecan-marshmallow streusel—are deeply rooted in tradition. These recipes, passed down through four generations, carry stories and memories. The chicken pot pie, with its flaky homemade crust, is a rite of passage; macaroni and cheese is a crowd favorite we perfected together, and cornbread dressing symbolizes our unity during the holidays, while sweet potato soufflé brings our family together to share stories while peeling sweet potatoes.

Family-style dishes encourage sharing and connection. Garlic-steamed mussels, lasagna, summer fish fries and fried chicken with sweet corn on the cob and potato salad all foster conversation as guests pass serving spoons and enjoy each other's company. These dishes naturally bring people closer, creating a sense of togetherness that goes beyond the food.

To serve large groups effortlessly and stay stress-free, consider delegating tasks or hosting a potluck-style gathering. Having family members bring their signature dishes lightens your load and makes everyone feel included. Set up a well-organized serving station, label each dish and prep in advance—chop vegetables, marinate meats and assemble casseroles the day before. Enlist help to plate meals or guide guests through the buffet line so you can relax and enjoy the celebration.

Adding small, thoughtful touches can elevate any gathering. Consider placing heirloom linens like your grandmother's embroidered tablecloth on the table. Include personal mementos like old family photos as conversation starters, and curate a playlist that resonates with older family members. Storytelling corners allow relatives to share family histories, creating a deeper connection to the food. Even simple themes or decor can leave a lasting impression.

In the end, hosting is about more than just the meal; it's about creating memories, sharing traditions and nurturing relationships. Whether you're accommodating dietary restrictions or celebrating multi-generational recipes, the goal is to incorporate love and meaning into every dish, turning an ordinary meal into an unforgettable experience. After all, some of life's most precious moments are shared around the dinner table.

Welcome To My Table

# HOMEMADE CHICKEN POT PIE
# WITH FLAKY BISCUIT CRUST

*Serves 4-6*

## INGREDIENTS

**Filling Ingredients:**

2 to 3 cups shredded roasted chicken

1 cup frozen peas

1 cup diced carrots

1 cup of chopped celery

1 cup diced small white or red potatoes

1 medium onion, chopped

2-3 cloves of garlic, minced

2 tbsp all-purpose flour

1/4 cup cognac or brandy (optional; you
can use extra chicken broth instead)

1 cup heavy cream

1 cup chicken broth

1 tsp dried thyme

1 tsp dried sage

Salt and white pepper to taste

**Biscuit Crust Ingredients**

2 cups all-purpose flour

1 tbsp baking powder

1/2 tsp salt

1/2 cup unsalted butter, cold and cut into
small pieces

3/4 cup chilled buttermilk

May substitute biscuit crust for puff
pastry.

## INSTRUCTIONS

1. Preheat your oven to 375°F(190°C).

2. In a large skillet over medium heat, sauté the onions, carrots, celery and potatoes until just tender, about 10 minutes. Add the garlic and sauté for another minute.

3. Sprinkle the flour over the vegetables, stir well and cook for another minute. This will help thicken your filling.

4. Slowly pour in the chicken broth, heavy cream and cognac (if using), stirring constantly. Bring to a simmer and cook until the sauce has thickened, about 2-3 minutes. If not using cognac, add an additional 1/4 cup of chicken broth.

5. Add the chicken, peas, thyme, sage, salt and pepper. Stir well to combine. Remove from heat and set aside.

6. For the biscuit crust, combine the flour, baking powder and salt in a large bowl. Cut in the butter using a pastry cutter (or your hands) until the mixture resembles coarse crumbs. Pour in the milk and stir until just combined. Do not overmix.

7. Turn the dough out onto a floured surface and knead it a few times to bring it together. Roll the dough out to about 1/4 inch thick and cut it to fit the top of your ramekins or casserole dish.

8. Pour the chicken mixture into your ramekins or casserole dish. Top with the biscuit dough.

9. Bake in the preheated oven for about 25-30 minutes or until the crust is golden brown and the filling is bubbly.

10. Let it cool for a few minutes before serving. Enjoy your home-made chicken pot pie with a flaky, biscuity crust!

PRO TIP:
Add a splash of white wine to the sauce for added depth of flavor. Add fresh herbs like thyme to biscuit dough for extra flavor.

SERVING SUGGESTION:
Pair with a crisp green salad for a balanced meal.

**Watch Video!**

**CHICKEN POT PIE**

**JUST JEANNIE**

Gather & Feast

# CREAMY SOUTHERN-STYLE MAC AND CHEESE

*Serves 8*

## INGREDIENTS

1 lb elbow macaroni

4 tbsp unsalted butter

1/4 cup all-purpose flour

3 cups whole milk

1 cup heavy cream

4 cups shredded cheese (cheddar, Monterey Jack, and Gruyère recommended)* for a deep and rich flavor, substitute Monterey Jack cheese with Smoked Gouda

1 tsp Dijon mustard

1/2 tsp paprika

Salt and pepper to taste

## INSTRUCTIONS

1. Cook macaroni until al dente and drain.

2. In a large saucepan, melt butter and whisk in flour to form a roux.

3. Gradually add milk and cream, whisking until thickened.

4. Stir in cheese, Dijon mustard, paprika, salt and pepper until smooth.

5. Mix the cheese sauce with the macaroni and transfer to a baking dish.

6. Top with more shredded cheese and bake at 375°F for 20 minutes.

## PRO TIP:
For extra crunch, sprinkle panko breadcrumbs on top before baking with or without crispy pancetta.

## SERVING SUGGESTION:
Serve as a hearty side or main dish with barbecue ribs.

Welcome to My Table

# SWEET POTATO SOUFFLE WITH MARSHMALLOW AND PECAN TOPPING

*Serves 8-10*

## INGREDIENTS

4 large sweet potatoes, peeled and boiled

1/2 cup unsalted butter

1/2 cup brown sugar

1/4 cup heavy cream

1 tsp cinnamon

1/4 tsp nutmeg

2 large eggs, beaten

2 cups of Marshmallows

**Pecan Topping:**

1 cup chopped pecans

1/2 cup brown sugar

1/4 cup flour

3 tbsp melted butter

## INSTRUCTIONS

1. Preheat oven to 350°F.

2. Mash boiled sweet potatoes with butter, sugar, cream, cinnamon, nutmeg and eggs until smooth.

3. Spread into a greased baking dish.

4. Sprinkle both the marshmallows and pecan topping over the top of the sweet potato mixture.

5. Bake for 25-30 minutes until topping is golden and crisp.

PRO TIP:
Add a splash of orange juice to the sweet potato mixture for a fresh twist.

SERVING SUGGESTION:
Perfect alongside roasted turkey or ham.

# TRIPLE MEAT BONANZA CHILI

*Serves 8-10*

## INGREDIENTS

1 tablespoon olive oil

2 medium yellow onions, chopped

3 cloves garlic, minced

3 tablespoons chili powder

2 tablespoons paprika

1 tablespoon ground cumin

2 teaspoons dried oregano

1/2 pound ground beef chuck

1/2 pound ground turkey

Shredded cheddar cheese and sour cream

4 mild Italian sausage links, removed from casings and crumbled

1-2 teaspoons salt (to taste)

2 28-oz cans crushed tomatoes with puree

1 15-oz can each of kidney, pinto, and barbecue baked beans, drained and rinsed

1-2 tablespoons minced chipotle chiles in adobo sauce (adjust to taste)

For the Garnishes, Tortilla chips

## INSTRUCTIONS

1. In a large pot, heat the olive oil over medium heat.

2. Add the onions and garlic, sautéing until they're soft, about 5-8 minutes.

3. Add the chili powder, paprika, cumin and oregano to the pot, stirring until the spices are well combined with the onions and garlic.

4. Add the ground beef, sausage and turkey meat to the pot, stirring and breaking the meat apart.

5. Add salt to taste. Increase the heat to medium-high and cook until the meat is browned, about 8-10 minutes.

6. Stir in the crushed tomatoes with puree and the drained beans. Add the minced chipotle chiles in adobo sauce. Reduce the heat to low.

7. Cover the pot and let the chili simmer for about 1 hour, stirring occasionally.

8. Taste the chili and adjust the seasonings if necessary, adding more salt or chipotle chiles as desired.

9. This Hearty Meat Chili is a warming, comforting dish, perfect for cooler weather.

# DESSERTS

*Welcome to My Table*

# CLASSIC SOUTHERN HUMMINGBIRD CAKE

*Serves 12-14*

## INGREDIENTS

**For the Cake:**

3 cups all-purpose flour

2 cups sugar

1 teaspoon baking soda

1 teaspoon ground cinnamon

½ teaspoon salt

3 large eggs, room temperature

1 cup vegetable oil

1 cup crushed pineapple, drained

2 cups mashed ripe bananas
   (about 4 bananas)

1 teaspoon vanilla extract

1 cup chopped pecans (plus extra for garnish)

**For the Cream Cheese Frosting:**

8 ounces cream cheese, softened

½ cup (1 stick) unsalted butter, softened

3 cups powdered sugar, sifted

1 teaspoon vanilla extract

## INSTRUCTIONS

1. **Prepare the Cake Batter:**
   Preheat oven to 350°F (175°C). Grease and flour three 9-inch round cake pans or line with parchment paper for easy release.
   In a large bowl, whisk together the flour, sugar, baking soda, cinnamon and salt.
   In a separate bowl, beat the eggs and vegetable oil until combined. Stir in the mashed bananas, drained pineapple and vanilla extract.
   Gradually fold the wet mixture into the dry ingredients using a spatula.
   Do not overmix—just stir until combined.
   Gently fold in chopped pecans.

2. **Bake the Cake:**
   Divide the batter evenly among the three prepared cake pans.
   Bake for 25-30 minutes or until a toothpick inserted into the center comes out clean.
   Let cakes cool in the pans for 10 minutes, then transfer to a wire rack to cool completely before frosting.

3. **Make the Cream Cheese Frosting:**
   In a large mixing bowl, beat the cream cheese and butter together until smooth and creamy.
   Gradually add the powdered sugar, one cup at a time, beating on low speed until fully incorporated.
   Mix in the vanilla extract and continue beating until light and fluffy.

4. **Assemble and Frost the Cake:**
   Place one cake layer on a serving plate and spread an even layer of frosting on top.
   Repeat with the second layer, then top with the final cake layer.
   Frost the top and sides of the cake evenly.
   Sprinkle extra chopped pecans on top for a decorative touch.

Desserts

Welcome To My Table

## PRO TIPS & TWISTS:

**Extra Moisture Boost:** For an ultra-moist cake, add ½ cup sour cream or ¼ cup buttermilk to the batter.

**Tropical Twist:** Add ½ cup shredded coconut to the batter for a more tropical flavor.

**Spice It Up:** Enhance the warmth with ½ teaspoon nutmeg or ¼ teaspoon ground ginger in the dry ingredients.

**Presentation Perfection:** Garnish with dried pineapple flowers or a drizzle of caramel sauce for an elegant touch.

**Storage:** Store the cake in an airtight container in the refrigerator for up to 5 days. Bring to room temperature before serving.

**Watch Video!**

HUMMINGBIRD CAKE

JUST JEANNIE

Desserts

# APPLE CRISP

*Serves 10-12*

## INGREDIENTS

**For the Crisp Topping:**

1 cup old-fashioned oats

1 cup all-purpose flour

1 cup packed light brown sugar

1/2 cup chopped pecans (optional)

1 teaspoon ground cinnamon

1/2 cup unsalted butter, melted

**For the Apple Filling:**

6 large apples (a mix of Granny Smith and Honeycrisp works well), peeled, cored and sliced

1/4 cup granulated sugar

2 tablespoons all-purpose flour

2 teaspoons ground cinnamon

1 teaspoon lemon juice

## INSTRUCTIONS

1. Preheat your oven to 350°F (175°C). Lightly grease a 9x13-inch baking dish and set aside.

2. In a large bowl, toss the sliced apples with granulated sugar, flour, cinnamon and lemon juice until well coated. Pour the apple mixture into your prepared baking dish and spread out evenly.

3. In another bowl, combine the oats, flour, brown sugar, pecans (if using) and cinnamon. Pour in the melted butter and stir until everything is well mixed and clumpy. Sprinkle this topping evenly over the apples.

4. Bake in your preheated oven for 40-45 minutes or until the apples are tender and the topping is golden brown.

5. Allow the apple crisp to cool for about 10 minutes before serving. It's delicious on its own, or you can serve it with vanilla ice cream or whipped cream.

**Watch Video!**

APPLE CRISP

JUST JEANNIE

Desserts

# LEMON CREAM CHEESE POUNDCAKE

*Serves 12-14*

## INGREDIENTS

### For the Cake:

1 ½ cups unsalted butter, softened to room temperature

8 ounces full-fat brick cream cheese, softened to room temperature

2 ½ cups granulated sugar

⅓ cup sour cream, at room temperature

2 teaspoons pure vanilla extract

½ teaspoon almond extract

½ teaspoon lemon extract

Zest of one lemon

6 large eggs, at room temperature

3 cups cake flour (spooned and leveled)

½ teaspoon baking powder

⅛ teaspoon salt

### For the Lemon Glaze:

1 cup powdered sugar

2-3 tablespoons fresh lemon juice

1 teaspoon lemon zest

1 tablespoon heavy cream or milk (for a smooth texture)

## INSTRUCTIONS

1. **Prepare the Oven and Pan:**
   Preheat the oven to 325°F (163°C).
   Generously grease a 10-12 cup Bundt pan with butter or nonstick baking spray. Ensure every crevice is coated to prevent sticking. Lightly dust with flour and tap out the excess.

2. **Make the Cake Batter:**
   In a large mixing bowl, beat the butter on high speed until smooth and creamy, about 2 minutes. Use a rubber spatula to scrape down the sides and bottom of the bowl.
   Add the cream cheese and beat on high speed until fully combined and creamy, about 1 minute.
   Add the sugar and beat on high speed for 1 minute, until light and fluffy.
   Add the sour cream, vanilla extract, almond extract, lemon extract and lemon zest. Beat on high speed until smooth. Scrape down the bowl.

3. **Add the Eggs:**
   Reduce to low speed and add the eggs one at a time, allowing each egg to fully mix before adding the next. Do not overmix after the eggs are added. Stop mixing after the 6th egg is incorporated.

4. **Add Dry Ingredients:**
   In a separate bowl, whisk together the cake flour, baking powder and salt.
   On medium speed, gradually add the dry ingredients to the wet ingredients, mixing just until combined. Do not overmix.
   Give the batter a final mix by hand using a rubber spatula to ensure there are no flour pockets or lumps at the bottom. The batter will be thick and creamy.

5. **Fill the Pan and Bake:**
   Pour or spoon the batter evenly into the prepared Bundt pan, leaving about 1 inch of space from the top.
   Gently tap the pan on the counter a few times to remove air bubbles.

Desserts

Bake on the center rack for 75-90 minutes or until a toothpick inserted into the center comes out clean.

6. **Cool and Remove from Pan:**
   Remove from oven and allow the cake to cool in the pan for 20 minutes.
   Gently run a butter knife around the edges to loosen.
   Invert the cake onto a wire rack and let it cool completely before adding the glaze.

7. **Make the Lemon Glaze:**
   In a small bowl, whisk together the powdered sugar, lemon juice, lemon zest and heavy cream or milk until smooth.
   If the glaze is too thick, add a little more lemon juice. If too thin, add more powdered sugar.
   Drizzle the glaze over the cooled cake.

## PRO TIPS FOR A PERFECT POUND CAKE:

**Room Temperature Ingredients:** Cold ingredients won't blend well—let butter, eggs, and sour cream sit out for at least 1 hour before using.
**Use Cake Flour:** Cake flour creates a lighter crumb than all-purpose flour. If you don't have it, make your own by substituting 1 cup of cake flour with 1 cup minus 2 tablespoons of all-purpose flour plus 2 tablespoons of cornstarch.
**Grease the Bundt Pan Properly:** Use butter and flour or a high-quality baking spray with flour to prevent sticking. Get into every groove.
**Do Not Overmix:** Overmixing once the eggs are added can make the cake dense and tough. Mix just until combined.
**Prevent a Sticking Disaster:** Let the cake cool in the pan for 20 minutes before inverting. If stuck, place a warm towel over the pan to help release it.

## STORAGE TIPS:

Store at room temperature in an airtight container for 3 days.
Refrigerate for up to 7 days. Bring to room temperature before serving.
Freeze for up to 3 months. Wrap tightly in plastic wrap and aluminum foil before freezing.

Desserts

# CELEBRATION PLATES

# CELEBRATION PLATES

Sometimes, a dish that you've carefully planned can take an unexpected turn, but with a little creativity, you can turn a potential setback into a memorable success.

One Thanksgiving, I had planned to serve a sweet potato pie, but in the midst of preparing multiple dishes, I accidentally scorched the sweet potatoes. Rather than panicking, I embraced the challenge and pivoted, roasting a sugar pumpkin I had on hand. I quickly whipped up a pumpkin cheesecake, and to my surprise, it became the star of the evening.

When it comes to crowd-pleasing recipes for festive occasions, there are a few that never fail to impress. My Garlic Herb Prime Rib is always a showstopper—it's beautifully roasted with a flavorful herb crust and serves as a dramatic centerpiece for the table. For gatherings with children or those who prefer lighter fare, my Spinach and Mushroom Lasagna is a hit. It's hearty, vegetarian-friendly, and perfect for feeding a crowd. These dishes work because they are visually stunning, cater to a variety of preferences, and are easy to serve in large portions, reducing the need for complicated plating.

Taking classic dishes and giving them a modern twist is one of my favorite ways to keep things exciting. For example, I elevate Mac and Cheese by blending smoked Gouda and Gruyère, topping it with crispy pancetta and panko breadcrumbs. Deviled eggs get a luxe upgrade with a touch of truffle oil and a garnish of crispy prosciutto or smoked paprika. For an elevated Chicken Pot Pie, I swap the traditional crust for flaky puff pastry, filling it with roasted chicken, pearl onions, mushrooms, and a creamy white wine sauce. A sprinkle of fresh thyme and nutmeg gives it extra depth. Another favorite is Citrus-Glazed Carrots with Pistachios—roasted heirloom carrots caramelized and drizzled with a tangy orange-honey glaze, then topped with crushed pistachios and fresh mint. The unique flavors and textures transform these dishes from comforting classics to exciting new favorites.

Balancing indulgent recipes with lighter, healthier options is key to creating a well-rounded menu. I like to offer a mix of dishes: for every rich, indulgent item, I include something fresh and lighter, like a crisp salad or a roasted vegetable platter. Portion sizes are also important—serve indulgent dishes in smaller portions while offering heartier servings of lighter fare. Incorporating vibrant vegetables, like a citrusy fennel and arugula salad alongside creamy mashed potatoes, brings balance to the meal. Fresh herbs, too, brighten up even the richest dishes, providing a refreshing counterpoint.

Lastly, every dish I serve carries a little piece of my heart. Whether it's a family recipe or something inspired by my travels, I try to include at least one dish with a meaningful backstory. For my children's birthday brunch, I served heart-shaped pancakes inspired by the ones my grandmother used to make for me. Guests loved hearing the story, and it sparked a wave of shared memories among the parents. Sharing the story behind each dish—whether it's through a quick anecdote or by allowing guests to assemble their plates in a personal way—helps make every meal a part of the celebration's story.

# MAIN DISHES

# GARLIC HERB PRIME RIB WITH RED WINE JUS

*Serves 8-10*

## INGREDIENTS

**For the Prime Rib:**

1 (5-lb) bone-in prime rib roast

5 cloves garlic, minced

2 tablespoons fresh rosemary, chopped

2 tablespoons fresh thyme, chopped

2 tablespoons olive oil

2 tablespoons Dijon mustard

2 tablespoons kosher salt

1 tablespoon black pepper

**For the Red Wine Jus:**

1 cup red wine (Cabernet Sauvignon recommended)

2 cups beef stock

1 tablespoon butter

## INSTRUCTIONS

1. **Prepare the Roast:**
   Remove the prime rib from the refrigerator at least 1 hour before cooking to bring it to room temperature. This ensures even cooking.
   Preheat the oven to 450°F (232°C).
   In a small bowl, mix together the minced garlic, chopped rosemary, thyme, olive oil, Dijon mustard, salt and black pepper to create a flavorful paste.
   Pat the roast dry with paper towels and rub the herb-garlic mixture generously all over the meat, ensuring even coverage.

2. **Roast the Prime Rib:**
   Place the roast bone-side down on a rack in a roasting pan. If you don't have a rack, place thick slices of onion or carrots under the roast to elevate it.
   Roast at 450°F for 20 minutes to create a flavorful crust.
   Reduce the oven temperature to 325°F (163°C) and continue roasting until the internal temperature reaches 130°F for medium-rare (approximately 1.5 to 2 hours).
   o For rare: 120-125°F
   o For medium: 135-140°F
   o For well-done: 150-155°F

3. **Step 3: Rest the Meat:**
   Remove the roast from the oven and tent it loosely with foil. Let it rest for at least 20 minutes to allow the juices to redistribute.
   While resting, prepare the red wine jus.

### 4. Make the Red Wine Jus:

Place the roasting pan on the stove over medium heat and add 1 cup of red wine. Scrape up the browned bits from the bottom of the pan using a wooden spoon.

Pour in 2 cups of beef stock and bring the mixture to a simmer. Let it reduce by half, about 10-15 minutes.

Whisk in 1 tablespoon of butter for a rich, glossy finish.

Strain the sauce through a fine-mesh sieve for a smooth consistency.

### 5. Carve and Serve:

Use a sharp carving knife to slice the prime rib into thick, even portions.

Serve with the red wine jus on the side.

Garnish with additional fresh rosemary sprigs for a beautiful presentation.

## PRO TIPS FOR SUCCESS:

**Use a Meat Thermometer:** A digital thermometer ensures perfect doneness without overcooking. Insert it into the thickest part of the roast, avoiding the bone.

**Let it Rest:** Resting the roast keeps the juices inside, making every bite tender and flavorful.

**Choose the Right Wine:** A dry red wine like Cabernet Sauvignon or Merlot enhances the jus with a deep, robust flavor.

**Save the Bones:** Leftover bones can be used to make a rich beef broth or stock.

## SERVING SUGGESTION:

Pair with creamy mashed potatoes, roasted Brussels sprouts or a crisp green salad for a complete meal.

This version ensures every step is clear and easy to follow while adding expert tips for a foolproof prime rib. Let me know if you'd like any further refinements!

# PAN-SEARED HALIBUT WITH LEMON BEURRE BLANC

*Serves 4*

## INGREDIENTS

**For the Halibut:**

4 (6-ounce) halibut fillets

Salt and black pepper to taste

2 tablespoons olive oil

**For the Lemon Beurre Blanc:**

½ cup dry white wine

(such as Sauvignon Blanc)

1 shallot, finely chopped

¼ cup heavy cream

½ cup unsalted butter, cubed and chilled

Juice of 1 lemon

## INSTRUCTIONS

1. **Prepare and Sear the Halibut:**
   Pat the halibut fillets completely dry with paper towels. Moisture prevents a crisp crust.
   Season both sides with salt and black pepper.
   Heat 2 tablespoons of olive oil in a large skillet over medium-high heat until shimmering.
   Carefully add the fillets to the pan and sear for 3-4 minutes on one side without moving them.
   Flip the fillets and cook for another 3-4 minutes until golden brown and the fish flakes easily with a fork.
   Remove from heat and let the fish rest while preparing the sauce.

2. **Make the Lemon Beurre Blanc:**
   In a saucepan over medium heat, combine white wine and chopped shallots.
   Simmer until the liquid reduces by half, about 5-7 minutes.
   Pour in heavy cream and simmer again until slightly thickened.
   Reduce heat to low and whisk in cold butter, one cube at a time, until the sauce emulsifies and becomes silky.
   Stir in fresh lemon juice and strain through a fine-mesh sieve for a smooth consistency.

3. **Serve:**
   Drizzle the beurre blanc sauce generously over the pan-seared halibut.
   Garnish with capers, fresh dill or parsley for a bright finish.

## PRO TIPS FOR SUCCESS:

**Dry the Halibut Well:** A dry surface ensures a golden, crispy crust when searing.

**Use Cold Butter for the Sauce:** This helps the beurre blanc emulsify properly, creating a rich and creamy consistency.

**Don't Overcook the Fish:** Halibut dries out quickly. Aim for an internal temperature of 130-135°F before resting.

## SERVING SUGGESTION:

Pair with steamed asparagus, roasted fingerling potatoes or a light citrus salad for a balanced meal.

Garnish with capers and fresh herbs like dill. Pair with steamed asparagus.

**Watch Video!**

PAN-SEARED HALIBUT

JUST JEANNIE

# HONEY LAVENDER ROASTED CHICKEN WITH CITRUS HERB BUTTER

*Serves 4-6*

## INGREDIENTS

1 whole chicken (4-5 lbs)

¼ cup honey

1 tablespoon dried culinary lavender

1 lemon, halved

1 orange, halved

**For the Citrus Herb Butter:**

½ cup unsalted butter, softened

2 tablespoons fresh herbs

  (chopped thyme, rosemary, parsley)

1 teaspoon kosher salt

½ teaspoon black pepper

## INSTRUCTIONS

1. **Prepare the Chicken:**
   Preheat the oven to 375°F (190°C).
   In a small bowl, mix softened butter with chopped herbs, salt and black pepper.
   Pat the chicken dry with paper towels.
   Using your fingers, gently loosen the skin over the breast and thighs. Rub half of the butter mixture under the skin and the remaining butter all over the outside of the chicken.

2. **Stuff and Glaze the Chicken:**
   Stuff the chicken cavity with lemon and orange halves to infuse flavor.
   Tie the legs together with kitchen twine for even cooking.
   In a small bowl, mix honey with dried lavender. Brush the honey mixture evenly over the chicken.

3. **Roast the Chicken:**
   Place the chicken on a rack in a roasting pan (or a bed of sliced onions for elevation).
   Roast for 1.5 to 2 hours, basting occasionally with pan juices.
   Check for doneness: The internal temperature should read 165°F in the thickest part of the thigh.
   If the skin browns too quickly, tent loosely with foil to prevent burning.

4. **Rest and Serve:**
   Remove the chicken from the oven and let it rest for 15 minutes before carving.
   Serve with roasted lemon halves for squeezing and garnish with fresh lavender sprigs.

Celebration Plates

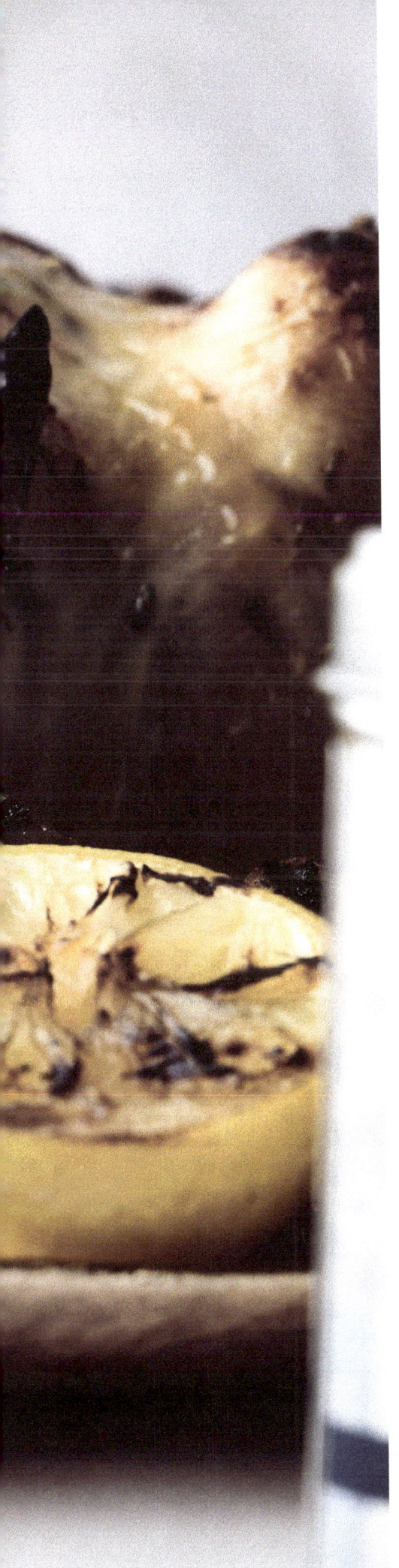

## PRO TIPS FOR SUCCESS:

**Loosen the Skin Carefully:** This ensures the citrus herb butter flavors the meat directly, keeping it moist.

**Let the Chicken Rest Before Carving:** This allows the juices to redistribute for a tender and juicy texture.

**Use a Meat Thermometer:** Insert it into the thickest part of the thigh without touching the bone for an accurate temperature reading.

## SERVING SUGGESTION:

Pair with roasted root vegetables, garlic mashed potatoes or a crisp arugula salad for a well-rounded meal.

**Watch Video!**

ROASTED CHICKEN

JUST JEANNIE

# SIDES

# CITRUS-GLAZED CARROTS WITH PISTACHIOS AND MINT

*Serves 4-6*

## INGREDIENTS

1 lb carrots, peeled and cut into uniform pieces (for even roasting)

¼ cup orange juice (freshly squeezed for best flavor)

2 tbsp honey

2 tbsp olive oil

¼ cup pistachios, chopped

Fresh mint leaves, for garnish

½ tsp salt

¼ tsp black pepper

## INSTRUCTIONS

1. **Preheat the Oven:**
   Set your oven to 400°F (200°C).

2. **Prepare the Carrots:**
   Toss the peeled carrots with 1 tbsp olive oil, salt and black pepper. Spread them in a single layer on a parchment-lined baking sheet.

3. **Roast the Carrots:**
   Roast for 20-25 minutes, turning them halfway through for even caramelization.

4. **Make the Glaze:**
   While the carrots roast, whisk together the orange juice, honey and remaining 1 tbsp olive oil in a small bowl.

5. **Glaze and Roast Again:**
   Drizzle the glaze over the roasted carrots and toss to coat.
   Return to the oven for another 5 minutes to allow the glaze to caramelize slightly.

6. **Garnish and Serve:**
   Sprinkle with chopped pistachios and fresh mint just before serving.

## PRO TIPS:
Use rainbow carrots for a vibrant presentation.
For extra crunch, toast the pistachios in a dry pan over medium heat for 2-3 minutes before adding them.
Want more depth of flavor? Add a pinch of cinnamon or a dash of balsamic vinegar to the glaze.

## SERVING SUGGESTION:
Serve on a white platter to highlight the bright colors. Pairs well with roasted meats or grain-based dishes.

Celebration Plates

Welcome to My Table

# HERB-INFUSED PARKER HOUSE ROLLS WITH HONEY BUTTER GLAZE

*Makes 16 rolls*

## INGREDIENTS

**For the Rolls:**

4 cups all-purpose flour

1 packet (2 ¼ tsp) active dry yeast

¼ cup granulated sugar

1 ½ tsp salt

½ cup whole milk, warmed (110°F)

½ cup unsalted butter, melted and slightly cooled (divided)

½ cup warm water (110°F)

2 large eggs

1 tbsp finely chopped fresh rosemary

1 tbsp finely chopped fresh thyme

1 clove garlic, finely minced

Flaky sea salt, for garnish


**For the Honey Butter Glaze:**

3 tbsp unsalted butter

2 tbsp honey

## INSTRUCTIONS

1. **Activate the Yeast:**
   In a small bowl, combine the warm water, yeast and 1 tbsp of sugar. Let sit for 5-7 minutes until foamy.

2. **Mix the Dough:**
   In a large mixing bowl, combine the flour, remaining sugar and salt.
   Add the yeast mixture, warm milk, ¼ cup melted butter and eggs.
   Mix until the dough begins to come together.

3. **Incorporate the Herbs:**
   Add the rosemary, thyme and minced garlic to the dough.
   Knead on a floured surface for 8-10 minutes (or use a stand mixer with a dough hook for 5-6 minutes) `until the dough is smooth and elastic.

4. **First Rise:**
   Transfer the dough to a lightly greased bowl. Cover with a damp cloth or plastic wrap and let rise in a warm spot for about 1 hour or until doubled in size.

5. **Shape the Rolls:**
   Punch down the dough and divide it into 16 equal pieces.
   Roll each piece into a smooth ball and place in a greased 9x13-inch baking dish or on a parchment-lined baking sheet.

6. **Second Rise:**
   Cover the rolls with a damp cloth and let them rise again for 30-40 minutes until puffed.

7. **Bake the Rolls:**
   Preheat the oven to 375°F (190°C).
   Brush the tops of the rolls with the remaining melted butter.
   Bake for 20-22 minutes or until golden brown.

8. **Add the Honey Butter Glaze:**
   While the rolls are baking, combine butter and honey in a small saucepan over low heat until melted.
   Brush the warm rolls with the glaze as soon as they come out of the oven.
   Sprinkle with flaky sea salt for an extra touch.

Celebration Plates

## PRO TIPS:

For even fluffier rolls, let them rise for a few extra minutes before baking.
Want a deeper flavor? Replace half the flour with bread flour for a chewier texture.
For a hint of spice, add a pinch of cinnamon or nutmeg to the honey butter glaze.

## SERVING SUGGESTION:

Serve these rolls warm with whipped herb butter or alongside soups and holiday mains.

**Watch Video!**

PARKER HOUSE ROLLS

JUST JEANNIE

# GRILLED VEGGIE PLATTER WITH LEMON HERB DRIZZLE

*Serves 4-6*

## INGREDIENTS

1 zucchini, sliced

1 eggplant, sliced

1 red bell pepper, sliced

1 yellow bell pepper, sliced

1 bunch asparagus, trimmed

2 tbsp olive oil

Salt and pepper to taste

**Lemon Herb Drizzle:**

2 tbsp olive oil

Juice of 1 lemon

1 tbsp chopped parsley

1 tsp chopped thyme

## INSTRUCTIONS

1. Preheat grill to medium-high.

2. Toss vegetables with olive oil, salt and pepper.

3. Grill vegetables for 3-4 minutes per side until charred and tender.

4. Whisk together, drizzle ingredients and pour over grilled vegetables.

## PRO TIP:
Add crumbled feta or goat cheese for extra flavor.

## ALTERNATIVE SEASONAL VEGGIES:
If certain vegetables aren't in season, substitute with:
o Summer: Corn on the cob, cherry tomatoes, pattypan squash
o Fall: Brussels sprouts, delicata squash, carrots
o Winter: Broccoli, cauliflower, sweet potatoes
o Spring: Snap peas, artichokes, radishes

## SERVING SUGGESTION:
Serve as a vibrant appetizer or side dish alongside grilled meats or fresh bread.

# SYTLE & SCENTS

# STYLE & SCENTS

One of my favorite tablescapes was for a Christmas gathering, where I chose not to do the traditional red and green and embraced a stunning, unconventional color scheme of navy blue, dark green, and black plaid linens. This unexpected palette felt fresh, elegant and sophisticated.

I layered two napkins at each setting—a solid navy one and a coordinating plaid napkin—secured with napkin rings I crafted from navy blue velvet ribbon adorned with sparkling embellishments. For the dinnerware, I chose my wedding china—Wedgewood ivory plates with gold and navy trim—and paired them with gleaming Wedgwood and Baccarat stemware, adding a touch of timeless luxury.

The centerpiece featured two lush floral arrangements with hydrangeas, red and white roses, gilded eucalyptus, cedar, pine and red berries, creating a rich, festive feel. To further elevate the ambiance, I used my Yuletide Balsam Whisper room and linen spray, filling the air with the crisp scent of fresh-cut pine. The warm glow of my Berry & Bough Scented Candles and soft Christmas music completed the experience, creating an atmosphere that made my guests feel like royalty—a goal I always strive for when hosting.

### Scent Matters at the Table
Dining is more than just taste—it's an experience that engages all the senses. Just as a well-curated tablescape enhances a meal, the right scent can transport guests, evoke memories and set the tone for an unforgettable gathering. The interplay between aroma and flavor has long been recognized, but intentionally pairing food with home fragrances can take your hosting to a new level of sophistication.

### Creating the Perfect Sensory Dining Experience
I subtly layer scents by combining candles and room sprays. Just before guests arrive, I spray my foyer with a fragrance that fits the occasion, which gives my space a quick boost. I then light a candle that complements the spray. This quickly makes my space feel amazing and inviting.

I don't want the aroma to compete with food, so I layer scents subtly by choosing lighter scented candles or room sprays or using just a spray or candle alone. I think it's important to use a fragrance as a prelude to welcome guests before serving a meal. It tantalizes the taste buds and sets the mood for the event.

Don't be afraid to incorporate natural elements like fresh herbs, dried citrus or cinnamon sticks in the centerpieces on your table. For Christmas, I used dried oranges wherever I could. The fresh orange scent permeated my home and added to the festivity of the season. Choose fragrances that align with the time of year for a seamless experience for your guests. For my Christmas tablescape, I found Yuletide Balsam Whisper with a combination of Berry & Bough, both by Pivotal Moments, perfectly aligned with my vision for my guests.

## How to Pair Food with Scents

Just like wine pairing, matching home fragrances with dishes requires balance. This can be done by incorporating scented candles and/or room linen sprays. Here's a guide to help you create the perfect ambiance for your guests through scent:

## Citrus & Fresh Herb Pairings:

Lemon verbena, zesty orange, bergamot, basil, rosemary and mint are invigorating scents that refresh the senses and mirror the zesty notes in foods. I find these scents work exceptionally well for brunches, as well as seafood and light pasta dishes.

## Floral & Delicate Notes:

Afternoon teas, garden parties and French pastries work well with scents of jasmine, honeysuckle, rose or lavender. These lighter scents add a sense of elegance that elevates delicate desserts and teas.

## Warm & Spiced Aromas:

Autumn and winter dishes require warm scents of cinnamon, nutmeg, clove, cardamom and vanilla. Best for fall gatherings, holiday dinners and hearty meals. These warm notes wrap your space in a warm and cozy way, making your guests feel right at home.

## Woodsy & Earthy Accents:

Pair scents like sandalwood, cedarwood, patchouli and smoked vanilla with grilled meats, rustic dishes and outdoor dining. These scents provide a grounding, rich aroma that complements the savory flavors of roasted and grilled dishes.

## Sweet & Gourmand Delights:

To elevate and indulge your sweet tooth, caramel, tonka bean, and roasted coffee chocolate is my go-to. These scents are perfect for dessert courses, coffee pairings and intimate dinners. They create a sensual and luxurious feel for your guests.

## Bringing It All Together

To transform a simple meal into something extraordinary, thoughtfully pair food with a beautifully curated tablescape and fragrance. Whether hosting a festive holiday dinner, an elegant brunch or an intimate evening for two, the right scent can elevate the ambiance, making every bite more memorable.

**Watch Video!**

SOULSCAPE

JUST JEANNIE

### Tips for Creating Tablescapes That Leave a Lasting Impression:

**Choose an Unexpected Color Scheme:**
Break away from traditional colors to add sophistication. For example, navy and dark green bring an elevated, modern feel to Christmas decor.

**Layer Textures and Details:**
Combine elements like patterned tablecloths, layered napkins and textured floral arrangements to create visual interest.

**Incorporate Luxurious Touches:**
Small details, like velvet napkin rings or heirloom china, can make a big impact.

**Set the Mood with Music:**
Music weaves together the mood of a gathering, setting the tone from the moment guests arrive. Soft jazz can create an intimate, relaxed ambiance, while an upbeat playlist energizes the evening. Just like scent and décor, the right music enhances the dining experience, making every bite and conversation more memorable.

**Combining Textures, Colors and Details:**
Start with a strong foundation, such as a textured or patterned tablecloth and layer complementary or contrasting elements. Plaid linens paired with solid napkins create depth and balance. Add interest with floral arrangements that mix large blooms, like hydrangeas and roses, with smaller accents, such as berries or gilded foliage. Finish the look with thoughtful details like shimmering stemware, candles and embellished ribbons to tie everything together seamlessly.

**Watch Video!**

TABLESCAPE

JUST JEANNIE

### Budget-Friendly Ways to Add Elegance:
Craft napkin rings from velvet ribbon and affordable embellishments like crystals and adhesive stripping found at a local craft store.

### Repurpose What You Have:
Use existing dinnerware, glassware or home decor items to create a polished look.

### Seasonal Greenery:
Combine greenery like cedar or pine with a few standout blooms to make lush floral arrangements without overspending.

### Reflect the Theme or Season:
Align your tablescape with the essence of the season. For Christmas, incorporate natural elements like cedar, pine, and berries for a winter wonderland vibe, and opt for rich, festive hues like navy and green. A seasonal scent, such as Yuletide Balsam Whisper by Pivotal Moments, adds cohesion, while curated holiday music ensures your table becomes an integral part of the celebration's story.

**Watch Video!**

NAPKIN RING TUTORIAL

JUST JEANNIE

# *With Gratitude*

I am deeply grateful to my mother, maternal grandmother, grandma Mamie, and my Aunties, Julia, Jeannette, Josephine and Zelia, for teaching me life-changing skills and values that continue to influence my journey. From an early age, they instilled in me the importance of cooking, cleaning, organizing and crafting beauty from even the simplest resources. By the time I was six years old, I could roast a turkey for our family Thanksgiving, bake pies, cakes and cookies, and create warm, welcoming spaces that bring people together. These lessons taught me the value of thoughtful preparation, creativity and connection, which have remained a cornerstone of everything I do.

Though my career as an OB-GYN was immensely rewarding, those early lessons always stayed with me, reminding me that nurturing joy and connection through food, decor and shared experiences is just as meaningful. Today, I'm thankful to use those same skills to celebrate life with my family and friends, creating traditions and memories that I hope will inspire my children and generations to come.

I also want to extend my deepest gratitude to my incredible publicist, Olivia Almagro, and my content creation crew, Amari & Co, Natalie and Candice! These ladies provided amazing support, creativity and dedication, elevating my brand and bringing my vision to life. Through their talent and hard work, they have helped me share my story in ways I could have only dreamed of, ensuring that every moment and creation is captured beautifully.

To you, the reader, your support and feedback have been invaluable in shaping the Just Jeannie brand. It's because of you that I've been able to share my passion and expand my vision for helping others find inspiration in the everyday. Through your encouragement, I've been able to evolve this journey into something far greater than I ever imagined.

As you explore the delectable recipes and designs within this book, I hope you'll make them your own. Use them to create new family traditions, celebrate milestones or simply elevate the beauty of your everyday moments. My greatest hope is that the lasting lessons in these pages will encourage you to savor life, embrace creativity and find joy in celebrating even the smallest occasions.

Let's continue this connection as you try these recipes and designs—share your creations, ideas and moments with me. Together, we can inspire one another and build a community rooted in creativity, warmth and celebration.

The key takeaway I want you to carry from this journey is that every moment, no matter how big or small, is worth celebrating. Through thoughtful touches, shared meals and intentional connections, you have the power to bring beauty and joy into your life and the lives of those around you. Thank you for allowing me to be part of your journey—it's a gift I don't take lightly.

**With love and gratitude,**
*Jeannie*

# Sources

Unless otherwise noted, tableware and linens are privately owned.

### Maison Gabrielle
Contributed all spices & seasonings
Maisongabriellefrance.com
Get 10% off your purchases with code:
JUSTJEANNIE

## Shop Now!

### Pivotal Moments
Pivotalmomentsbyjj.com
Candles and room sprays

## Shop Now!

### Amari & Co
Tablescape photography, page 173
Videography, page 177
@amari_and_co
Photographer and Videographer:
Natalie D'Onofrio

### Baccarat
Baccarat.com
800 221 6330
Fluted stemware

### Cat on The Table
Food Photography and Video
@cat_on_table
Catontable.es

### Wedgewood
Wedgewood.com
China and Wine Glasses

### Solino Home
3753 Howard Hughes Parkway
Suite 200-707
Las Vegas, Nevada 89169
solinohome.com
Table linens

### Central Market
3815 Westheimer
Houston, TX 77027
713-386-1700
Centralmarket.com
Floral Centerpieces

Welcome to My Table